SVEN MARTIN

A huge thank you to all the people who made this book possible –
to the contributors, helpers, friends, supporters and readers.

Publishers: James McKnight, Ben Winder
Editor: Marcela Bonells
Designers: Chris Jones, Harriet Jones
Research: Morgane Charre
Tea: Archie Bromfield
Production: Theo Fellgett
Photography: Sven Martin, Sebastian Schieck, Boris Beyer
Contributors: Kike Abelleira, Marcela Bonells, Morgane Charre,
Scott Edgworth, Matthew Fairbrother, Siddharth Gandhi,
Iago Garay, Francesco Gozio, Paul Humbert, Léo Kervran,
James Lumley-Parkin, Andy Lund, Anka Martin, James McKnight,
Ric McLaughlin, Miranda Miller, Romain Paulhan, Dan Roberts,
Mike Rose, Christian Textor, Ines Thoma, James Vincent

Supporting brands: Mondraker, Pivot Cycles, Santa Cruz,
YT Industries, Forbidden, Schwalbe, Maxxis, Fox Racing

Yearbook mega fans*: Matthew Dewey, Joel Duthie, Simon
Everitt, Patti Fellgett, Yanick Garon, Tim Grant, Zach Heaton,
Thomas Loitesberger, Andrew Marcaccio, Roderick Powolny,
Andy Reid, Philip Rojan, Adam Samardzija, Yorick van den Ingh,
Vincent Zagula

*These people ordered the Finders Keepers pre-order bundle that
we hid on our website for only our biggest fans to find. Thank you
to them and to you too.

Cover image: Sven Martin

Published by Misspent Summers
Printed by Cambrian Printers, Wales

misspentsummers.com
finalework.space

Tamed Rebel

When reflecting on the 2023 Enduro World Cup season, it's best first to take a deep breath, hold it, exhale.

A lot and not much changed in the year enduro became recognised and managed by cycling's international governing body, the UCI, and Warner Bros. Discovery, the international media megacorp behind Eurosport, CNN, and *Tom & Jerry The Movie*.

You could say the sport's very essence took a slight turn as the Enduro World Series (EWS) was renamed the Enduro World Cup. Or EDR for short, the awkwardness of the official acronym perhaps symbolic in some way – maybe enduro didn't like being packaged into someone else's spreadsheet.

At the same time, and despite much worry for racers, teams, brands and fans pre-season, when the reborn EDR arrived in Tasmania for the season's opening races, the future looked bright. Spectators in their thousands lined Maydena's and Derby's stages, the racing action came thick and fast, a host of superstar downhillers joined the enduro ranks and the event branding looked better than ever. Those races were brilliant.

The season was split into three distinct blocks of racing: block one in Tasmania; block two in Italy and Austria; block three in France. There were months-long breaks between each stint of events – time for racers to reflect and regroup, modify their training; an opportunity for the organisers to evaluate their successes and failures and adapt accordingly.

Block two was perhaps a tough point in the year for everyone involved. Round four of the series in Leogang, Austria, should have been a step into the spotlight for enduro as it lined up alongside downhill and cross country at an event billed as a festival of mountain biking. Alas, it seemed like a bit too much had been crammed into the week's schedule and enduro fell into the shadows of its better-known brethren. There were no ill intentions – we're sure the organisers meant for the best and the dream was to push enduro to a new audience; it just didn't work out quite that way. Nonetheless, the racing was fast-paced and exciting.

But by the end of the year things were coming back together and the season ended on a high with some of the best-ever race stages at the final round in Châtel, France. That event was low key but the racing was awesome; the year ended with one of the tightest series battles we can remember in both the men's and women's categories.

As much as it pains us to say it (we're massive racing fans and we appreciate the efforts of every person running the series), if you look at social media or below any website posts, you could easily get a pretty dismal view of the 2023 EDR season. But people generally comment online when they have something critical to say; this might skew the general perception of how well the series did during the year. As Pivot Factory Racing's Eddie Masters noted in our newsletter after the last round of racing, 'The pieces of the puzzle are all still there, just somewhere along the line everything's been muddled up. We're only a few key moves from putting it all together.'

From where we were standing, enduro racing in 2023 looked as promising as ever. There were some glitches, but we think they were simply the growing pains of a sport on its path to maturity.

We hope you enjoy going through the photos and reports in this book and look forward to seeing you at a future race.

– James McKnight

CONTENTS

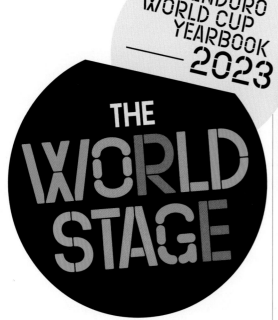

ENDURO
WORLD CUP
YEARBOOK
—— 2023

THE WORLD STAGE

52-73

78-99

100-121

ROUND 1: MAYDENA, AUSTRALIA

ROUND 2: DERBY, AUSTRALIA

ROUND 3: PIETRA LIGURE, ITALY

128-149

150-171

176-197

202-223

228-251

The Third Act

Words: Ric McLaughlin. Image: Sven Martin

The UCI Enduro World Cup was built on foundations laid in place a decade ago.

It was my first Enduro World Series (EWS) race day, and the Whakarewarewa Forest was drenched. It was so wet that the water had seeped inside my clothes. I could feel a channel trickling between my shoulder blades, snaking down my spine and into my shorts. Like overwatering a house plant, the water poured so intensely that the ground couldn't absorb it fast enough. It felt like it was bouncing back up around me.

It was also my first day using a video camera professionally, and it had long since stopped working. A pick-up truck pulled up alongside me. I handed the waterlogged Sony A7S to one of our helpful production team members, who fiddled with it for 20 seconds before declaring, 'Yeah, it's fucked', with a smile. I was out of my depth and sinking. The bike race was thundering on through the trees around me, and I had no idea how I would cover it.

The next day, drier but now accompanied by a towering hangover acquired under the shelter of Rotorua's covered walkways, I sat down with several spreadsheets and a box of paracetamol to try to untangle the stories. Cécile Ravanel, as was her fashion, had won seemingly at a canter, and Wyn Masters had clinched victory by cleverly not crashing. In contrast, everyone else had succumbed to toppling off somewhere along the line. Lensless goggles, a good couple of inches of chin dribble and kit soaked black with mud, Masters had cut a bashful figure on the podium the previous evening.

Back then (2017), the EWS was at the zenith of its individuality. It had boldly strolled forth from the twin towers of mountain bike broadcasting and struck out on its own. It had first invented and then galvanised a new all-conquering genre of bikes and equipment. It was still weird and unrefined, growing, morphing and shifting, if at a slightly reduced rate than during the opening years of its gestation.

As the years have passed, from a seat inside the shuttle, it feels as if it has brought mountain bike racing into its orbit rather than the other way around. Its awkward teenage years began by demanding individuality before finding respect among its peers. Acceptance is the final phase.

The UCI World Cup in Loudenvielle-Peyragudes will be seen as a significant moment in enduro racing's history. For the first time, it solely shared a gravity weekend alongside its decades-older stablemate, downhill. In Leogang, earlier in the same year, it had also been on equal footing with Cross Country Olympic and Cross Country Short Track. With such auspicious company often comes the insecurity of your legitimacy and right to be there. The only star of a solo show can suddenly feel like lesser billing in the stadium.

But it's not. Enduro has a trump card that no other format can touch. It's perhaps the truest form of mountain bike racing. Most of the mountain bikes leant up in the sheds, garages, and workshops are now capable of racing an enduro. A few psi in the tyres and some lube on the chain, and they're good to go. They are not extravagant, one-trick indulgences or specialist race tools for the affluent or competition-obsessed. The EWS' cleverest legacy was to self-sustain by reproducing the bikes best suited for racing it. In most countries, enduro has taken on the mantle of the all-important grassroots race scene. These bikes are what people race because these are the bikes that they ride.

It's grandiose to suggest that a sport involving bicycles worth several thousands of pounds is in any way working class, but just as some of the greatest musical acts, sports stars and cultural icons have come from a place of the people, speaking like the people, so too does enduro. Enduro racing is mountain biking – endure the ups to harvest the downs.

From the weird, rambling explanations of the early days, the two helmets, the thousands of broken rims and the parties in the piazzas, enduro is here to stay. Against all odds, it has blossomed into a UCI World Cup. Soon, it will have a UCI World Championship set of rainbow stripes, at long last, too.

Without spoiling what is to follow, the first season of the UCI Enduro World Cup came down to the last stage in both elite categories. Enduro has never been a finished product. Every year, there are tweaks and changes aimed at making it better, but in its first full season as a top-flight format, its stars produced for its fans its best season to date. That fact is indisputable and alludes to a future glittering with unpredictability and intrigue. Enduro racing has arrived, but what it does next will continue to captivate us in the language we all speak.

"From the weird, rambling explanations of the early days, the two helmets, the thousands of broken rims and the parties in the piazzas, enduro is here to stay"

Notes from UCI EDR World Cup Round 1 in Maydena, Tasmania:

- Many of the top gravity riders have been down in Queenstown, New Zealand, lately, including a number of top EWS – sorry, EDR – racers
- While most of the downhill racers and freeriders headed over to Crankworx Rotorua, the enduro specialists and one or two downhillers headed to Tasmania for this first-ever UCI EDR MTB WC race
- **End of EWS**: 2022 marked the tenth season of Enduro World Series racing, and its last. ESO Sports, the EWS organiser, and Warner Bros. Discovery are organising the entire mountain bike World Cup series in 2023 – including enduro, which is now an official UCI World Cup discipline and part of the, er, MTB World Series
- Check out **Cosmic**, our 2022 EWS film, for free here
- Oh yeah, we made this book for ESO to celebrate a decade of EWS racing (see what we did with the name?)
- **2022 recap**: Jesse Melamed and Isabeau Courdurier won the final EWS series after hard-fought battles and plenty of thrills and spills during the season
- There are six stages at the Maydena EDR, all of which will be raced on Sunday (the Pro Stage has been shelved for 2023)
- The action kicked off with some riders opting to walk sections or entire tracks (Maydena has 820m vertical elevation so walking the entire race course would've been tough on the hooves)
- Then on Friday they headed out to practice the **long and varied stages**. There is a lot to remember – Maydena has a huge array of trails and terrain and the race stages are taped wide so learning the lines will be key to a good result. Many GoPros will be watched
- Check out our Squids On Tour course preview video by Sven and co here. Careful, it's a lot of fun
- Side-note: not sure we'll ever get used to typing EDR
- **Bike checks etc**: Check out Moir and Melamed's new rides in a video by ESO here*
- *And watch our recent interview with Jesse here
- About Maydena Bike Park: Well, it's simply brilliant and surely up there with the world's best official riding destinations? Check it out for yourself here
- **Schedule recap**: Amateur race on Saturday. Pro race on Sunday. The action kicks off at 09:00 Aussie time. Full schedule here
- **Broadcast info**: ESO will be putting out a short event highlights video straight after racing and then a longer video next week including all the action (much like they produced for the EWS races – there won't be any live broadcast). Look out for both on the MTB World Series and new GMBN Racing YouToob pages
- **Weather**: Looks to be a spot cloudy but otherwise rain-free all weekend
- Downhillers racing EDR Tasmanian [sic] include **Vali Höll, Troy Brosnan and Connor Fearon**. They've all raced enduros in the past so it's good to see them back for more
- **Vibe**: Good times and the riders mostly seem mostly excited that enduro is now a World Cup discipline
- **Coming up**: We'll have interviews and photo galleries on our Instagram this weekend and then an online **zine-thing** during the week
- If you haven't already got our 2022 yearbooks, there are still some copies available on our store, plus plenty of other stuff. Your support is greatly appreciated
- Thanks for reading and stay tuned!

Notes from Derby, Tasmania, UCI Enduro Mountain Bike World Cup Round 2:

- Check out our Squids On Tour Derby course preview video here (well worth watching)
- **Quick recap** on last week's race: Isabeau Courdurier and Luke Meier-Smith opened the 2023 enduro season with wins in the elite categories on Maydena Bike Park's amazing trails
- It was an Aussie 1-2-3 in the men's race
- Emmy Lan and Sascha Kim took the U21 wins
- Full results from Maydena here. Also, we made this points calculator. Does it work?
- Please take a minute to check out our online zine, podcast-thing and more on the Scraps section of our website. Lots more coming next week
- This week's **racing in Derby is on Saturday** (things kick off at around 11pm central European time on Friday – any Europe-based night owls staying up to follow the live timing? See you there)
- International enduro last visited Derby in 2019 for the second round of the Enduro World Series
- That race was also in late March and racers were treated to some late-summer sunshine and good times. Which brings us on to:
- Weather report: Err um yeah. Liquid sunshine on and off all week so far. **Practice day was a mud bath** and there's a spot of rain forecast for Saturday's race
- Terrain: Mud in places, sandy elsewhere and plenty of big, grippy boulders all over the place
- Status: The end of **stage six has been most affected** by the weather. It's a flat, muddy, sticky slog and in Friday's amateur race almost nobody made it through the two-minute-ish section – most had to dismount and push
- Some EDR racers have **asked for the section to be removed** for the main race – we'll soon find out what the organisers decide
- **Length**: It's going to be a tough day out with long, winding singletrack uphills and a decent chunk of altitude – 1,400m climbing officially but a few hundred metres more according to some racers' Garmins
- Liaisons: The set times for **pedalling between stages** were deemed a tad optimistic by racers during practice, so the organisers have added a little time to the liaisons – it'll still be a hard day in the office though
- Grit: The six race stages are long and winding with a mix of **fast hits through boulder fields and plenty of flat sprints.** The race will likely be won on a mix of technical ability and stamina – sounds pretty enduro to us
- Vibe: Despite the changeable weather, everyone's having a great time on Derby's fantastic trails. Another destination to put on the must-visit list. Check out the Ride Blue Derby website for more info here
- **Videos:** Check out the official videos here – raw practice action included
- Coming up: Interviews and galleries on our Instagram this weekend and then another online zine and podcast-thing during the week
- If you like what we do, please support us by going on our store, sending a tip from the footer of our website or simply telling your friends about us. More eyes on our stuff helps an enormous amount
- **Thanks for reading** and stay tuned!

Notes from Finale Outdoor Region, UCI Enduro Mountain Bike World Cup Round 3:

- **Finale Ligure, Finale Outdoor Region, or Pietra Ligure?** Finale and Pietra are neighbouring towns and are both part of the wider Finale Outdoor Region area
- Traditionally, racing has happened every year since 2013 in Finale Ligure, except for in 2020 when one of the Covid double-header Enduro World Series rounds was held on Pietra Ligure's trails. This year, **the main pit area and racing is in Pietra**
- One thing that hasn't changed is the quality of **ice cream.** Gelateria Pastorino in Calice Ligure is our temple
- **Full event preview, squid style:** Check out the trails, banter and beaches in Sven's Pietra Ligure video here
- **Fan action:** Organisation has put out this neat spectator map showing the stages and where to watch the racing
- **Official practice video** here
- 2023 season so far: It's been quite a while since rounds 1 and 2 in Maydena and Derby, Tasmania, so you might want to **refresh your memory** of those races with our online zines here and here and 'Views podcast-things here and here
- Read the **full official lowdown** and find rule books, start lists, etc on the MTB World Series website here
- Not just enduro: There's also an **XC Marathon World Cup** on Sunday. The race sets off from Finalborgo (Finale's quaint old town) on a 100km mission around the mountains with nearly 4,000 metres of climbing and an array of technical descents. Nutters
- Where's the party? A hot topic this week is where everyone's going to celebrate after the race – Pietra or Finale?
- Talking of endurance, **the EDR looks set to be the toughest of the year** so far, with six stages comprising a total 2,070m climbing and 3,105m descending (there's one big shuttle at the start of the day), plus 56km total on-bike distance
- There's a mix of two really long (4km and 6km) stages and four short ones (all under 2km)
- Feedback from riders after Thursday's practice day is positive – good, varied, mostly fun stages. But some of the trails have lots of tricky, tight turns that are hard to judge speed on and easy to mess up
- Doing well here means going flat-out in rocky sections, getting a good rhythm through long series of corners, and keeping it clean. There aren't any notable uphill slogs or sustained sprints in stages
- **Weather check:** Scorchio! There's been some rain this week, but the trails will likely be dry for racing
- Beaming at you from Finale Work Space this week – our office in Finale and coworking hangout thing. Drop in for a tea if you're ever in the area
- Teams and brands are **a bit scattered about** as some booked accommodation in Finale (about five mins' drive from neighbouring Pietra) in advance, assuming the race would be there
- Did a local guide offer to show riders the race tracks for money weeks before the course map was made public?
- We are already hard at work on our 2023 EDR and DH World Cup yearbooks (The World Stage and Hurly Burly). This year we're putting things together during the season so we can print and post them much earlier than ever before. Stay tuned for behind-the-scenes stuff and pre-orders starting soon
- This Friday and weekend is a national holiday in Italy, celebrating the country's Republic Day. That means lots of people in the area and hopefully a lot of spectators for the racing
- **Series leaders:** Coming into this race, Richie Rude and Bex Baraona lead the men's and women's elite series standings. But the points are tight at the top and a good (or bad) result here could flip the top-six in either category
- In the **2020 EWS in Pietra,** Adrien Dailly and Mélanie Pugin took the elite wins. Who's your money on this time?
- **Thanks for reading** and stay tuned on misspentsummers.com for lots more stuff this year

Tennis elbow: Notes from Enduro World Cup #4 in Leogang, Austria

- As with all the EDR races this year, this is a **one-day race with six timed stages** and physically challenging transfers between the stages
- **Start lists and other information** can be found on the MTB World Series event page for Leogang <u>here</u>
- Riders **practiced the course on Wednesday** and racing is today, Thursday 15 June
- **Terrain check:** Lots of berms. Dust and holes. High speeds. Some nice natural stuff in the woods
- **Plus some freestyle course marking** taking riders off main bike park lines into off-cambers and other fun diversions
- Watch the official **practice video** <u>here</u>
- **Weather check:** Mostly sunny with clouds
- **Vibe check:** Light moaning with intermittent positivity
- There have been some **grumbles** about the tracks and course marking, but most riders seem to be getting on with the job and enjoying themselves. Despite an abundance of machine-built stuff, there's loads of decent tech in the woods
- **Race day:** Riders leave from Leogang on Thursday morning before transferring over to Saalbach, another ski resort on the other side of the mountain
- En-route, they swing by <u>Spielberghaus,</u> a hotel in the hills famous for the person who grew up there. Nope, nothing to do with filmmaking! Downhill World Champ Vali Höll was raised in this very place and learnt to ride bikes on the nearby slopes
- The first **three stages are in Saalbach.** Stage two is one of the better trails of the day
- Then riders **head back to Leogang** using much of the same root-infested transfer trail but in reverse. We rode this yesterday and found it, err, less jiggly on the return
- The final three stages are on Leogang's **bike park slopes** and criss-cross the hill to access some sections of earthy, rooty, hand-cut trail and lots of machine-built berms, oodles of dust and a good helping of braking bumps
- Stage six is a fast blast down **part of the old downhill track,** starting from after the big wooden wallrides and ending in the resort's famous arena
- Racing starts late and the **final stage will be at around 8pm** for the top elites
- Check out the course map <u>on Trailforks here</u>
- **Official course stats:** 70.9km distance*, 4,726m climbing**, 4,696m descending***
- *Including chairlifts
- **Nobody seems to know what percentage is pedalling and what is on the lifts – riders skipped a big transfer in practice and could access all the trails using the ski-lift network, so they don't have their own stats; the information isn't readily available without doing some high-level mathematics
- ***We're not sure **where the other 30m went** (the course starts and ends in the same place in Leogang)
- There's also an official <u>course map graphic here</u>
- Stages two and three are absolute beasts. S2 is physical and S3 covers more than 700m of descending
- If you're wondering why riders mostly chose to **drive around to Saalbach** to practice the three stages there instead of pedalling the transfer to find out what they'd be up against in the race, they probably wanted to save their energy as there isn't a rest day between practice and racing like there has been at other rounds this year
- There is **one tech-feed zone** during the race. It was going to be in Leogang but has been moved to Saalbach, so teams must zip around there (about a 45 mins drive) and set up ready for riders to drop in and fuel up after stage three
- **Hot tip for parched mechanics:** If you find yourself at a loose end and famished in Saalbach, Bäckerei Unterberger serves a mean cream and strawberry croissant and coffee. For savoury tastes, try the cheesy swirly pastry thing. For more culinary recommendations, please dial 1-800-GLUTTONS
- Unlike in downhill and cross-country, **course marking** doesn't appear to have changed since 2022 – tape is still needed to ensure nobody misses turnings or cuts corners. Having said that, tapes are only

in place where it seems absolutely necessary. We're all for reducing the amount of plastic strewn around

- **E-EDR:** There's also e-bike enduro racing here. Ex-downhill World Champ Fabien Barel has announced he isn't not making a comeback after all. Barel won the first E-EDR in Pietra Ligure a couple of weeks ago but only planned to race that one. But then he couldn't resist the urge to try his luck again here
- Legend **Tracy Moseley** is back racing E-EDR too
- **Other stuff:** As well as EDR and E-EDR practice, Wednesday was also junior downhill practice; on Thursday, as well as the enduro, there's junior downhill qualifying, elite downhill practice, and under-23 cross-country short track finals
- **Series rankings: Jesse Melamed** leads the elite men's EDR by 18 points with 1,070 points coming into Leogang. **Morgane Charre** and **Isabeau Courdurier** are level pegging with 1,231 points in the elite women's but Charre will carry the leader's jersey here as she most recently won an event (<u>Pietra Ligure</u>)
- **Fabien Barel** and **Laura Charles** lead the E-EDR series after winning in Pietra
- It's going to be a busy week in Leogang! Stay tuned for more from the enduro and downhill racing coming up
- <u>Boris</u>, <u>Sven</u> and <u>Seb</u> are out here snapping all the best photos for <u>The World Stage</u> and <u>Hurly Burly</u>. Thanks to them for the hard work and Sven for the photos in this email and to you for reading!

THE GOOD STUFF: Notes from Val di Fassa, Italy, Enduro World Cup (EDR) R5

- **Quick season recap:** The EDR started with rounds one and two in <u>Maydena</u> and <u>Derby</u> in Tasmania before heading to <u>Pietra, Italy</u>, and then <u>Leogang, Austria</u>, last week
- **Series leaders:** Richie Rude (USA) and Isabeau Courdurier (FRA) lead the elite rankings before Val di Fassa. Sascha Kim (AUS) and Emmy Lan (CAN) lead the under-21 points
- EDR Val di Fassa (VDF) start lists and other official stuff <u>here</u>
- Today's EDR and E-EDR will finish a lot earlier than the Leogang round – riders were still on course after 8pm there. This time the last riders are scheduled to finish at 17:30
- **Eddie Masters' videos are pure gold.** Check out his practice and bike weigh-in videos <u>here</u> and <u>here</u> for the best action and commentary. We also love following Jack Moir's <u>Moi Moi TV</u> and <u>Jesse Melamed's course previews</u>
- Every race so far this year has had six stages (always on a single day of racing). VDF has *only* five, but it sure ain't going to be an easy day out. Across 44km distance there's well over 1,000m of climbing and around 3,000m of forearm-destroying descending
- **Lifts make the difference:** Riders make use of VDF's impressive ski lift network (8 lifts and 18 trails open to mountain bikers in the valley) to gain massive height (peaking well over 2,000 metres) before plunging back down on long, physically demanding stages
- There's also the electric **E-EDR** which takes in eight stages over about 400m extra vertical and 6km extra distance
- There are some **brutal climbs in stages.** Previously in VDF the organisers have used an untimed 'neutral zone' to cancel out a lung-and-leg-busting climb mid-stage. This year, the open race had a neutral zone on a stage but the pros just have to get their heads down and sprint to infinity and beyond. This long endurance climb should suit the fittest, most powerful riders – it's a place to win some serious time
- The official spectators map page on the <u>FassaBike site here</u> has a decent breakdown of each stage
- You can also check out the course map on Trailforks <u>here</u>. Fancy giving it a go?
- Follow the **live timing** on the MTB World Series site <u>here</u>. Select the category you want to see then check the individual stage results and the overall race leader/results (cumulative time adding each stage time together). But...
- ...the 'Overall' tab shows the current race ranking and automatically updates as each rider finishes a stage. As every rider must finish the stage to know who is in the overall race lead, the current overall is usually misleading (because there are usually still riders on stage). If you're lucky, you can click on the 'Overall' tab and select a stage number to scroll through the progression of the day's results,

seeing who was leading after each stage. But this function rarely seems to work for us – do you have the same problem?

- If you're wondering, the official event name is Val di Fassa, but **everyone calls it Canazei** because that's where the event village is
- **The venue:** Towering mountains, huge descents, enormous pizzas. The Dolomites at their best
- **Vibe check:** Upbeat. Riders like this venue – its long and natural trails are a world away from Leogang's whackerplated berms (although, despite some initial grumbles, most riders really enjoyed Leogang)
- **Conditions check:** HOT and sunny. There were big storms forecast during practice which led to the session being split across two days instead of the planned single day of practice. In the end it wasn't as bad as predicted, but the trails did take a dousing, making for slick conditions for Thursday and Friday practice. The sun's been out and the trails should all be griptastic for racing
- **More practice time** = more pushing up riding stuff again. While riders are still only allowed a single run on each track, a bit more time in the schedule means they have been able to stop and inspect sections and push back up to try new lines. Will this affect the results?
- **Tangent:** It's a busy week for eventing, with Crankworx Innsbruck and <u>Stone King Rally</u> also happening. We'll have coverage from both in our next print publications (Spent 2 or/and Downtime EP)
- Oh, and Eurobike! We were there midweek for two days of cruising Frankfurt's exhibition halls checking out what's new. Our **full 2024 trends report in brief**: more e-bikes; burgundy paintjobs galore; sustainable, reusable, recyclable marketing copy aplenty. It was good to see **lots of downhill and enduro World Cup bikes** on brands' stands – the pointy end of mountain bike racing is as important and exciting as ever
- **Whispers from Eurobike:** We know this isn't enduro related content (ERC), but rumours travel fast when you get the entire bicycle industry in one place. You've probably heard about the industry over-stock crisis (brands, distributors and retailers got a bit excited with their order quantities during the Covid bicycle boom. Now things have slowed down drastically they're left with either massive excess inventory or bills they can't pay – or both). Unsurprisingly and unfortunately, it sounds like some big bike companies will be going deeper into full crisis mode or even shutting down completely by the end of 2023. We wish everyone the best of luck navigating the tricky times ahead
- **Anyway, back to the EDR:** We've been enjoying the official coverage this year. The <u>EDR VDF raw practice video is here</u> and is well worth a watch
- International enduro has been visiting VDF since the first Enduro World Series (EWS) here in 2019. This is the **fifth VDF EWS-EDR race** – there wasn't a race here in 2020 but there were two EWS rounds back-to-back in 2021, plus the 2019 and 2022 ones
- There are lots of trails in the area, but **all of the EDR stages this year have been raced before.** Any predictions based on previous performances here?
- The open race was on Saturday and took in stages 2-5. Check out the <u>results here</u>
- **Use your ears** to check out our 'Views Leogang podcast-thing (downhill only) by Sven Martin <u>here</u>. You can find it on Spotify too (search Misspent Summers)
- **We're a tiny company** finding our way and trying out different media stuff to complement our <u>downhill and enduro yearbooks</u>. Let us know if you have any feedback or ideas by replying to this email
- **Final tangent:** What is a bike park, anyway? Val di Fassa (raw, natural, rooty, earthy, rocky) has a very different interpretation than Leogang (some of that, but mostly berms, jumps, rollers). Both destinations refer to themselves as bike parks. Just a bit of random pondering
- **Thanks for reading!** We hope you are enjoying these notes emails. We're currently working on our 2023 yearbooks plus a load of other stuff including <u>Spent</u> 2 and some new clothing. Stay tuned for more! Cheers

FRESH notes from Loudenvielle Enduro World Cup

- As mentioned, ESO Sports, the series organiser, made the decision to **move the EDR race to Friday** from Saturday (as it was scheduled) to dodge bad weather forecast for the weekend. Riders seem happy with ESO's willingness to adapt the plan – lightning on Saturday could mean closed chairlifts and dangerous conditions

- About the schedule change, ESO said: 'This safety decision has been made to ensure the welfare of the athletes, teams, marshals, volunteers, spectators, and everyone working at the event'

- **This first combined enduro and downhill** World Cup (Leogang had cross-country too) pairs the gravity disciplines and puts them together in the perfect setting for a standout event with teams and riders mingling, enough space for both to shine, and world-class tracks for both races. Plus, non-stop action for visiting fans. Love it – bring on more events like this

- EDR racing kicked off with rider rollouts from the pits **starting just after 08:00** this morning, Friday 1 September. The final rider (Richie Rude) is scheduled to start the last stage at 17:36 – it's a long day of racing action in the Pyrenees

- Loudenvielle's EDR race consists of **five technical stages across 37km and over 3,000m of descending**. There's a range of challenges: from pinning it flat-out on widely marked stages through the meadows up high to tight and twisty technical tests (total tongue twister) down low. There's grass and ruts and loam and rocks and mud and roots. Basically, it's pure mountain biking and probably most people's idea of *proper enduro*

- There's 12 minutes of **hard-charging raw practice action in** this video

- Alex Rudeau, who won the EWS here in 2022, **talks through the race stages** in this course preview video

- **Blue sky thinking:** Conditions couldn't be better for racing today – sunshine, not too hot nor too cold, the trails have had some rain but not too much. Good move by ESO bringing the race forward by a day

- **Last time here in 2022, both elite categories (men and women) were won by flat pedal riders** (Rudeau and Misspent Summers' very own Morgane Charre)

- **Festival vibes:** Loudenvielle's local organiser sure knows how to throw a party – there are various side-shows all week (exhibitor stands, trials displays, DJ sets, signing sessions, a film night and more)

- If you're in the area, don't miss Friday night's **concert by freestylin' slopestyler Thomas Lemoine (aka** LIL MOINE)!

- Did a media representative get punched and knocked to the ground by an irate member of the public on recce day?

- **Shakedown shakeup:** Something missing in 2023 is the shakedown day that for the last few seasons has given pro riders a chance to hit a few laps of a track (not a race stage) a day before official practice with media crews trackside to document and publicise what's going on. This week especially feels like there's a bit less pre-race action being communicated out, despite various groups of riders staging their own informal shakedowns

- On the other hand, the new-for-2023 media conferences seem to be popular and get decent airtime for select racers. We didn't spot any EDR-ers or E-EDR-ers at Loudenvielle's press conference but to be fair they probably needed a spot of rest after practice

- It's been a while since the last EDR, so **here's a quick recap of the season so far:** The Enduro World Cup started in March with the first two rounds back-to-back in Maydena and then Derby, both in Tasmania, before a two-month break and then rounds three, four and five in Finale Outdoor Region, Italy; Leogang, Austria; and Val di Fassa, Italy

- **Out of five EDR rounds, there were three different pro women winners** (Isabeau Courdurier, Bex Baraona and Morgane Charre) **and five different pro men winners** (Luke Meier-Smith, Richie Rude, Jesse Melamed, Rhys Verner, Matt Walker)

- **The enduro series leaders** before Loudenvielle: Richie Rude (elite men), Isabeau Courdurier (elite women), Lisandru Bertini (U-21 men), Emmy Lan (U-21 women). Series rankings here

- Loudenvielle's enduro action kicked off on Thursday with practice day sending riders up both sides of the valley using a mix of pedal power, a gondola, a chairlift and a van shuttle. Everyone seemed to enjoy the stages

- **Full schedule** including rule books and start lists are on the MTB World Series site <u>here</u> (scroll down). Elite start times <u>here</u>
- **Ready, steady, wait a minute, go:** If you have a start list from Thursday and are wondering why it doesn't align with people's starts today, there was a **start lists update** at 11pm on Thursday night, changing some racers' start times by 30 minutes or more
- **There are also the amateur Open EDR and E-EDR events taking place today.** The e-bike race has had a stage lopped off (down to seven stages) to avoid any trail clashes with the open racing
- **Reliable timing here:** Brush up on your French and <u>follow the live timing on Trailow</u> if the official race feed isn't working. Trailow also offers, er, MTB uplift services across Europe
- **Iago Garay is back** on track following the terrifying brain aneurysm he suffered at round three in Finale Outdoor Region. Garay isn't racing but he's enjoying being team manager and managing to <u>out-style the entire field</u> despite his recent health scare. Great to see you riding again, Iago
- **EDR 2023 is like three seasons in one,** with months-long breaks between the three batches of racing (#1 Tasmania-Tasmania; #2 Italy-Austria-Italy; #3 France-France). There were major changes in the frontrunners between parts 1 and 2 of the season; what effect might the summer break have had on results this time?
- Several racers seemed to **pass through remote Loudenvielle by complete chance** during the summer. Who spent the longest in the area?
- **Useless ponderings #1,895:** What about releasing the map of race stages a few months in advance (instead of a week before the event) and setting up wildlife cameras on each track to make sure nobody gets accidental extra practice? Locals and visiting riders would then know which trails to steer clear of, putting competitors' minds at rest. Plus, it could lead to some fantastic nature imagery. Can't see any flaws in this plan
- Don't forget this year there are **points available for every race stage** – the overall race result is still decided on combined times (every stage time added together), but in 2023 racers also earn extra series points for their result on every stage. Consistency counts more than ever
- **#nightbro?** Enduro finishes early evening and elite downhill qualifying has also been shifted from its scheduled Saturday afternoon slot to Friday late afternoon (starting at 16:40) to avoid the forecast storms. Could make for some epic #lightbro photo conditions
- Watch the **official EDR highlights video** and other enduro #content for free (no paywalls here) on the <u>MTB World Series YouTube page</u> after the event
- Enduro **results** and interviews will be <u>on our website</u> after racing
- **Final note from us:** We love following and covering mountain bike racing and want to keep improving what we do. If you have any feedback about how to better our newsletters and <u>yearbooks</u>, please let us know by replying to this email or leaving a message on our <u>Trustpilot page</u>. Thank you for your support!
- **Also, big thanks to our yearbook photographers** <u>Boris Beyer</u>, <u>Sven Martin</u> **and** <u>Seb Schieck</u> (Sven took all the photos in this email) for running around capturing the best images and stories for us all year. Cheers!

PROPER notes from Châtel Enduro World Cup
With help from Pivot Factory Racing's Morgane Charre and Ed Masters

- **Enduro World Cup (EDR) Châtel** took in seven brutally technical stages across a 60km course comprising 800 metres of climbing and 3,600 metres of descending (the rest of the climbing was chairlift assisted)
- Basically, a lot more down than up, with no massive climbs or lengthy pedalling liaisons
- Riders were unanimous in their **praise for the trails** and the course overall. Rooty, loamy, dusty, gritty, grimy, slippery, hardpacked, loose, muddy, easy, hard, treacherous – there was something for every taste
- For the uninitiated spectator (and the initiated, for that matter), it wasn't obvious how to follow the race as riders travelled across several mountains in three distinct valleys. Finding start times, course maps, access routes, etc was a job for a forensic detective. Is that just the nature of enduro or could someone help the organiser create a simple platform for fans? Let us know if you have an idea

- Anyway, once you were on the stages and away from a few naysayers in the pits, there was **nothing but good vibes**, amazing riding and positivity. Riders, team, media, fans were loving the challenging stages
- It was cool to see the full pits set up at Châtel's Pré la Joux bike park – big Shimano booth, Nissan test drives (**we forgot to have a go**), nice event branding, etc. There weren't masses of people about, but it looked cool and the event ran smoothly as ever
- Internet rumours and truths say multiple racing teams (across all disciplines) will be disappearing in 2024. **Financial implosion** is an industry-wide issue, not the fault of any race organiser or event and certainly not limited to enduro. Regardless, there will probably be fewer professional contracts next year, but riders and fans will keep the spirit alive through a tough patch and things will pick up again soon
- Listen to this Downtime Podcast episode for some insight into industry struggles
- Enduro racing has **morphed and adapted over the 11 seasons** since the first Enduro World Series, with bikes, components, kit and riders adjusting to the format changes
- **Here's what a 2023 enduro bike looks like,** based on the top-three men's and women's bikes in the EDR series rankings*: 161.6mm rear suspension travel (average); 91.667% 29er (only 1 out of the 12 wheels was 27.5in); 1/3rd flat pedals (2 out of the 6 riders use flat pedals); made by YetrekPivLaComyon (six different brands took each of the top-three spots across both categories)
- The open enduro category continues to draw big entry numbers: in Châtel, there were over 300 riders entered into the open EDR and E-EDR categories
- **Alongside the enduro race,** there was also a slalom, a marathon World Cup (100km over the mountains in under five hours – ouch) and an unofficial jump jam that got shut down
- There was also the race to get your coffee orders in at Wood Café – the world's top racers were there daily all week mingling with fans, media and unsuspecting locals
- **Total tangent:** If you like BMX, check out Greystoke Magazine. It's new and old and we just got our copies – love it. Also, get yourself a copy of Cranked #34 – sadly the last one ever

*Based on the bikes they were using at the end of the season and our dodgy research

- **Isabeau Courdurier and Richie Rude** started the day leading the elite series standings by decent margins. But, with points up for grabs on every stage, it was still all to play for. Both riders would need solid results to secure the titles
- Morgane Charre (who, if you didn't know, is part of this company) got down to business and set about attacking the varied trails. **Charre and Courdurier went head-to-head all day,** exchanging stage wins (Hattie Harnden was the only other woman to win a stage) and the overall race lead as the day progressed – it was some of the tightest, most exciting racing we've seen in a long time
- On stage five, **Charre and Courdurier got exactly the same time** – down to the hundredths. Bonkers
- Going into the final stage of the day, the result could still go any direction. But Charre put in a strong ride to leap ahead and win the race by nearly seven seconds from Courdurier in second and Harnden third
- The final **series rankings saw Courdurier take the win,** her third EWS-EDR title, with Charre second and Harnden third. Congrats, all!
- **Watch the race highlights** here. We think the coverage in this final highlights vid of the season is the best of the year. Hats off to the producers – great filming, edit and energy. The follow drone footage and split screen stuff is awesome too
- If a tree falls in the woods: As Romain Paulhan sped through the final sections of stage three, a 30-metre-high pine tree came crashing down, falling between two groups of spectators directly into the track. Everyone rushed to clean things up and the debris were cleared before causing any riders trouble. Lucky it didn't fall on anyone – we were there and it was scary!
- The men's race was just as hard fought as the women's:
- **Jesse Melamed started the day with a stage win** and continued his attack from there, racking up four stage wins out of seven. He pushed hard until the end, also winning the last stage and taking the race win by more than 11 seconds. Melamed finished second in the season standings
- **Alex Rudeau finished his season on a high,** taking second place in the race and his fifth podium of the year. That put him third in the series overall

- Despite being the **winningest male in enduro history by far** with 19 Enduro World Series/Enduro World Cup wins (Melamed is the closest to Rude in total wins with 8 including Châtel), Rude hadn't scored a series title since 2016
- But, despite being slightly off the pace early in the day, Rude picked it up to finish third on the day and take the series title
- This latest series win makes it **three total titles for Rude**, equalling Sam Hill with the most EWS-EDR men's series wins
- Courdurier has racked up the series titles in a more compressed timeframe than Rude, with 2023 being her third series win after her 2019 and 2022 titles. That puts Courdurier equal with Tracy Moseley and Cécile Ravanel with three titles each
- Châtel also marked **Courdurier's 50th career EWS-EDR podium**. Respect
- Melamed and Courdurier have been racing enduro since the very start – both riders **raced the first EWS series back in 2013** and have been committed to 'duro ever since (they are the only riders in the top-three who have been there since the beginning)
- Did an E-EDR racer take an extra chairlift by accident?
- **Size matters or a matter of perspective?** At Châtel's podium celebrations, the same <u>football World Cup-esque trophy</u> was handed to each series winner then retracted and shielded from any champagne splatters before being carefully put back on its stand by its handler, ready for the next champion to lift in celebration. Later, each winner was given a scaled down version of the trophy to take home. Apparently, the winners' names from every discipline (EDR, XC, DH) will be inscribed on the big dog's base – but whose mantlepiece will it adorn?
- Charre and Courdurier weren't the only racers with exact same times on the day. In the men's, **Slawomir Lukasik and Dan Booker had identical race overall times**, both finishing exactly 24.860 seconds behind Melamed in the results. Nuts
- Under-21s racing was tight too: Simona Kuchynkova won the U21 women's race **by just one tenth of a second** and Raphaël Giambi took U21 men's by under two seconds
- Emmy Lan took a clear series win in U21 women with **nearly twice as many points** as her nearest rival. Second place went to Elly Hoskin who broke her foot in practice but had enough points to hobble onto the series podium in front of third-placed Lily Planquart
- **Lisandru Bertini's** raw speed carried him to win the U21 men's title just ahead of Raphaël Giambi in second and Sascha Kim in third
- **Florencia Espiñeira Herreros** and **Fabien Barel** wrapped up the E-EDR series titles
- What a season of enduro racing! We're currently putting it all into design for the next edition of <u>The World Stage</u>, which will be available on pre-order soon. Thank you for your purchases – they keep our wheels turning so we can do stuff like these newsletters and <u>films like Cosmic</u> (should we do another one this year?)
- Our pop-up downhill photo exhibition in Les Gets was such a success we nearly did a last-minute **enduro-specific pop-up** in Châtel, until we realised we totally didn't have the time or resources. How does a photo show and hang-out this December at our <u>Finale base</u> sound? More on that soon
- Thank you to Morgane Charre and Eddie Masters for the help putting together this newsletter. Hope you've enjoyed it! Cheers

FOR NOTES FROM RACING AND MORE SIGN UP TO

THE MISSPENT SUMMERS NEWSLETTER –>

MIS
SPENT
SUM
MERS

LONG LIVE CHAINSAW

JACKSON GOLDSTONE
MONT-SAINTE-ANNE WINNER
WORLD CUP OVERALL #2

THE DO IT ALL BIKE

Details that make all the difference. Differences that show character. **A character that can only be found in the DNA of Mondraker.** The FOXY CARBON is the enduro bike which encompasses all of the genetic identity of each and every one of our most successful competition bikes. That's how we've managed to define the mountain that can do whatever you ask of it, really well.

MONDRAKER.COM

SPENT
2021

BICYCLES AND DIRT ACTION

SPENT II

2022-2023

bicycles and dirt action

MOI

MOI

.......................I..II..............III.............I..WE.LIKE.DAT.SHIIEEETT

CONTENT SUPPORTED BY YT INDUSTRIES

LANDING IN THE MOB
SIAN A'HERN'S WORLD CUP RETURN

Following her 2016 junior World Cup overall and a series of select elite World Cup rounds, 2019 saw Sian A'Hern step away from competition. Fast forward several years, a sea of format shifts and a changed landscape, and in 2023 Sian returned to the sharp end of the sport, racing a World Cup season with factory support from the YT MOB.

MISSPENT SUMMERS: IN 2019, YOU STEPPED AWAY FROM COMPETITIVE DOWNHILL. WHAT LED TO THIS DECISION?
Sian A'Hern: The financial impact was a deciding factor, along with my love for racing just not being there anymore. I felt burnt out from trying to make it in the sport, never feeling as though I was closer to getting the team support I needed to build momentum with my racing. With multiple top-ten results, I felt deflated being declined, time after time. Taking a breather from the sport felt like my only option.

MS: SO, WHAT BROUGHT YOU BACK?
SA: I spent a few years at home working, discovering who I am and what makes me happy. I needed the time to figure it all out. Unfortunately, right as I planned to step back into racing, I suffered a brain injury. It put a pause on that for another year. Then, in August 2022, it all changed. I got the call from YT Industries to join them at Crankworx Whistler, meet the team, and get back between the tape!

To come second behind Tracey Hannah at my first race back was epic. The entire crew was waiting at the finish as I crossed the line, and my brother Kye landed in third in the men's event. It was overwhelming. Then, I raced Crankworx Cairns and landed in second again, only 0.1 seconds behind Tracey. I followed this up by taking the Taniwha DH win at Crankworx Rotorua... and that decided it for me. I needed to return to World Cups.

Then, the phone call came through, and everything changed. YT wanted me on the team for 2023, complete with full factory support. It was finally happening. It still feels surreal.

MS: WITH NEWCOMERS, A FRESH FORMAT, AND NEW TRACKS, WHAT STANDS OUT AS HAVING CHANGED IN YOUR ABSENCE?
SA: So much has changed in my time away. For starters, the women's field is stacked – I can name 20 girls who could podium or come close to it in any given race. It's awesome to see how strong and competitive the field is.

The new format has made for a super crazy year. With so many internal changes to our sport, it's mad adjusting to the new format as I step back into racing. Other than that, it's the same old scene, with only some minor changes you would expect over time.

MS: YOU LANDED WITH THE YT MOB – HOW DOES IT FEEL TO BE ON A FACTORY TEAM, AND HOW DOES IT IMPACT YOUR RIDING?
SA: I am honestly so grateful to have the support of the YT MOB. They're not just any team; these guys believe in me and my potential. It's insane how I only need to focus on riding and racing. Having the behind-the-scenes aspects covered by the team takes the pressure off, and having the support and love around you when racing makes it all so special. The MOB is such a good crew, and I am over the moon to be a part of it all. It's a little girl's dream come true!

MS: WHERE DO YOU STAND ON THE CURRENT STATE OF WOMEN'S DOWNHILL?
SA: Women's downhill is at an all-time high. Honestly, the level within the field is insane – just qualifying is HUGE. I'd love more finals spots for us girls to reflect this. The new Discovery changes are a step in the right direction; it's awesome that our feedback helps the sport move forward and improve for everyone, including the fans. We have a long way to go, but it's great to see changes having an impact.

MS: IF YOU COULD CHANGE ONE THING IN DOWNHILL, WHAT WOULD IT BE?
SA: Being away from racing for so long, I see things differently now. There are aspects of the culture I feel could benefit from change. I think the industry is quite stuck in its ways, and for me, being part of a team that thinks outside the box opens so many unique opportunities.

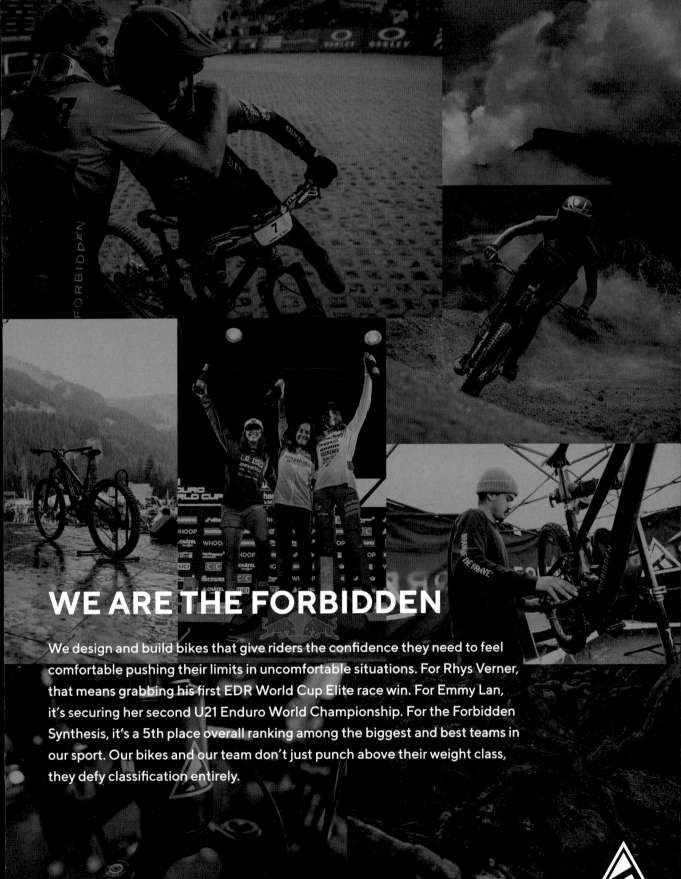

WE ARE THE FORBIDDEN

We design and build bikes that give riders the confidence they need to feel comfortable pushing their limits in uncomfortable situations. For Rhys Verner, that means grabbing his first EDR World Cup Elite race win. For Emmy Lan, it's securing her second U21 Enduro World Championship. For the Forbidden Synthesis, it's a 5th place overall ranking among the biggest and best teams in our sport. Our bikes and our team don't just punch above their weight class, they defy classification entirely.

forbiddenbike.com

FORBIDDEN™

WE'RE GONNA NEED MORE MOUNTAINS

VALENTINA ROA SÁNCHEZ: JUNIOR WOMEN'S CHAMPION
JACKSON GOLDSTONE: 2X ELITE MEN'S WINNER
MARINE CABIROU: 2X ELITE WOMEN'S WINNER
NINA HOFFMANN: 1X ELITE WOMEN'S WINNER

MAXXIS
TREAD VICTORIOUSLY

A PLACE WHERE YOU MAKE YOUR IDEAL LINE THE FINISH LINE

—

Get there

getthere.schwalbe.com

MORGANE CHARRE
1st Place Châtel EDR World Cup
2nd Place Overall UCI EDR World Cup

Misspent Sum
ternational gro
ists, photograp
ers and dropou
mountain bike
newsletters, c
zines, stuff, thi
positively and
Visit us online
summers or in
nale Work Spa

mers is an in-
oup of journal-
phers, design-
uts producing
media, books,
lothing, prints,
ngs and vibes
responsibly.
@misspent-
person at Fi-
ce.

Misspent Summers is an international group of journalists, photographers, designers and dropouts producing mountain bike media, books, newsletters, clothing, prints, zines, stuff, things and vibes positively and responsibly. Visit us online @misspentsummers or in person at Finale Work Space.

EUCI
ENDURO
WORLD CUP

TASMANIAN

SHIMANO

vittoria

prOxiM

UCI

EUCI
MOUNTAIN BIKE
WORLD SERIES

SVEN MARTIN

≡UCI
ENDURO
WORLD CUP

SHIMANO

vittoria

próxim

≡UCI

≡UCI
MOUNTAIN BIKE
WORLD SERIES

MAN

Modern-Day Transitioning

Words: Scott Edgworth. Image: Mike Rose

No, not like that. I'm talking about the crossover from little wheels to big ones.

BMXers swapping over to mountain bikes has been happening for years, but I never thought I'd be one of them. The small-wheeled friend is a great start for a life on bikes. It took me and my friends around the world, taught me things like discipline and determination, helped me develop bike skills and introduced me to many people. I managed to get towards the upper end of the sport, first with racing, then switching focus to the trail-riding side of things.

Our lives were often intertwined with mountain bikers back then – winters training in California or sharing dirt jumps at bike shows. It was a different era (around the turn of the century), and let's face it, mountain biking was still figuring itself out a bit. Looking back, I never really witnessed mountain biking in its natural habitat. I would see riders at the dirt jumps or watch the odd four cross race and didn't get it.

The first time I watched some proper mountain biking, I was fortunate enough to flick on the BBC showing Champéry Worlds and, in particular, 'That Run'. I was certainly excited and intrigued by this but didn't do anything about it then. A few years later, I got a call from an old friend. Kye Forte had started riding mountain bikes a few years prior and was on a road trip. He asked me to meet him in the Forest of Dean (FOD) because he had a spare bike and thought I'd enjoy it. This call led to a new chapter for me.

As you get older, you learn more about things like luck and appreciation. If I had gone on my own to try mountain biking, I would have ridden around aimlessly looking for tracks, running 60psi in my tyres while wearing a pair of Dickies. But the sport of mountain biking and its people are something special, and I want to highlight some of my experiences.

I had been away from bikes for a few years, but strong emotions were reignited with the familiarity of two wheels under me and an amazing crew, and that day really started things on a fortunate path. We rode with current downhill World Champ Charlie Hatton and World Cup racer Rich Thomas. I was fast-tracked into a sport that I knew nothing about. Instead, I was introduced to the FOD scene through Charlie and his brother Sam and immediately began riding with friends I'm still riding and racing with today. I was helped with bike set up, towed into tracks and welcomed with open arms.

The sport of mountain biking is still progressing. The top end is becoming more professional and elite. With the arrival of e-bikes, more people are enjoying the sport than ever, and I hope it can keep its accessible and welcoming nature. I can't think of many other sports where you are likely to share an uplift and maybe even ride with your heroes of the scene on the very first day.

Starting something new in your mid to late thirties is daunting as it's easy to feel you're on borrowed time. The obvious thing would have been to bring my BMX skills to a big bike, but instead, I wanted to immerse myself and learn new things. It's easy to rush the process at first. I could go fast but had no idea what to do when things were going wrong, which they inevitably did.

It has taken a few years to learn how to use a front brake, look at a track for braking points instead of features to pump, and let the suspension do its job instead of trying to make a full suspension bike feel like a BMX. It feels fun to learn and rewarding when you do. I've had to accept that I'll never be at the pointy end of this sport, but I have had some success along the way in both downhill and enduro. These opportunities are much more appreciated these days.

Nothing compares to riding 5- to 15-minute mountain stages incorporating everything from ridge lines to long loamers. That has been my motivation for travelling to the World Cups the past couple of years to race enduro. So, who knows what next years will look like? But being in the fortunate position of travelling and having an understanding family and the support of some great brands, I will be searching for those amazing tracks in the mountains.

It's just nice to feel grateful. At 43, I feel very lucky, but maybe the buzz is shifting from chasing the stopwatch to chasing my kids down the trail instead.

Thanks, mountain biking!

You Are The Sport

Words: Christian Textor. Image: Boris Beyer

Here I am, walking past some of the greatest people in our sport – Steve Peat, giving me a nod, Loïc Bruni triumphantly waving his arms in the air amidst the French crowds, the GOAT Greg Minnaar flying past, Sam Hill tearing apart that legendary 2008 Val di Sole track, and many more amazing events and people from past to present. I'm in the Misspent Summers's pop-up photo exhibition in Les Gets, getting carried away by some of the coolest moments of the sport captured in photography. I'm in awe of all these heroes of the sport that I love so much.

Their achievements are remarkable, and their stories are inspiring, constantly pushing the limits. This has led me to ponder about my place in all of this and whether I add anything special to this sport. The deeper I dig in, the more I realise that this sport and its heroes thrive due to the collective contributions of everyone involved. Behind these narratives, many people contribute to the sport in diverse ways – team staff, family, sponsors, volunteers, trail builders, mechanics, media and, obviously, racers.

If there weren't so many people racing for a less glamorous result on paper, fighting their battles to make things happen, pushing their limits and chasing their goals and dreams, the pointy end of things wouldn't have the same value, would it?

Yes, the winners and fastest get celebrated, and for good reason. However, it is equally fantastic to recognise that every racer has an exciting and eventful race, too, and sometimes even crazier.

I love hearing about other racers' stories after or throughout race day. Sharing thoughts, emotions, fears, and joys is one of the best things about racing and one of the greatest takeaways.

Often, I can tell when people are not happy with their performance; their self-confidence wanes, doubts start to creep in, and they can't help but feel less valuable. Suddenly, they feel their role is no longer important to the sport. I can see that with myself sometimes, too, and maybe that keeps us pushing and trying to improve as athletes, but there's definitely a fine balance to it.

Comparison is the essence of competition – comparing times in our case. But comparing the stories leading to the results doesn't make sense because unique things can't be ranked, and comparing them diminishes their value.

I tell myself repeatedly that 'I can do it because I am someone, and I don't have to do or accomplish something to be someone.' There's great freedom in that if we take it to heart, but it's not an easy task in a competitive sport, being a competitive person.

In my case, I found myself getting frustrated at times because I saw other racers training and riding all year round in perfect spots. At the same time, I could only squeeze in my riding at home – at non-World-Enduro-level tracks – between changing diapers and doing excavator jobs. I knew I would have to race these guys, which took the fun out of it before the race started.

That way of thinking can take the joy away from anything in life. I absolutely love my family, and I've chosen this lifestyle, knowing that balancing riding and racing wouldn't be easy. However, it's a pity to let negative thoughts take away your focus and overshadow the fun of the process – being at home, riding on home trails and racing against the world's best – because all I can think about is my potential disadvantage against other racers without knowing their struggles and challenges.

Come to think about it, this is a pretty counterproductive perspective. Racing bikes with these diverse people and their unique stories converging at the races is truly incredible. I absolutely love it and wouldn't trade this experience (and my circumstances) for anything in the world.

I can achieve something and add value because of who I am, even with all my fears and flaws. That amazes and motivates me to give it my very best. Obviously, I love riding and racing my bike, and that is my main motivator, but it's nice knowing that my contribution matters in the larger context of the sport, and so does yours.

"Often, I can tell when people are not happy with their performance; their self-confidence wanes, doubts start to creep in, and they can't help but feel less valuable"

The Genetics Of Athletics

Words: Kate Lawrence. Image: Siddharth Gandhi

Nurture vs nature is genetics' great cliché dilemma – a '29-inch vs 27.5-inch' for biology. But like all dilemmas that cause fierce debate, this is compelling because there is no correct answer. Are you racing or jibbing? Depending on the context, either answer can be correct. A person's background profoundly impacts their ability to become an elite athlete. Still, economic barriers and access and equity issues can limit the opportunities for pursuing that path.

However, when Isabeau Courdurier wins another overall title, or Jackson Goldstone wins a Downhill World Cup at age 18, one wonders how they got there. Was Courdurier born with something special? Did the hundreds of strider bike laps on the way to kindergarten shape Goldstone into the rider he is today? Is it nature or nurture that makes these athletes who they are?

Scientists have some answers. Our nature is encoded into our DNA – a series of four letters (amino acids) that create the complexity of all life on earth. The twin study is a favourite tool of geneticists to understand the 'heritability' of a trait – the extent to which variations in people's DNA account for differences in their traits. Identical twins have (almost nearly) the same DNA, while non-identical twins share only approximately half their DNA, like siblings. We can compare identical and nonidentical twins to figure out heritability.

Many athleticism-related traits have high heritability. For instance, VO2, a rough measure of endurance-type athleticism, has a heritability of ~45%.[1] The trainability of VO2 max, which doesn't correlate to baseline VO2 max (at least in mice), has a heritability of ~50%[2]. The heritability of elite athlete status is estimated at ~65%.[3]

DNA encodes this information in many ways, but the most important is storing the instructions to make specific proteins. Proteins are the little machines that do most of the necessary things to keep you alive and functioning. The instructions for each protein are stored on a part of the DNA referred to as that protein's gene. Different people will have variants (different DNA letters) in their genes, and these differences can cause the gene to make different versions of the protein.

To determine how nature plays into sports, we want to determine which gene variants might make you a better athlete. One way to do this is by breaking similar genes in mice and studying what goes wrong. This is like trying to figure out how a bike works by hitting your bike with a hammer and noting what goes wrong the next time you go out for a ride. When you put a huge dent into the stanchion of your fork, you'll find that the bike doesn't absorb bumps nearly as well. So, you can conclude the fork stanchion must be important for bump absorption. This approach identified 14 genes associated with running and swimming endurance in mice.[4] While this can help us identify genes important in athletics, it doesn't tell us much about which variants might make someone a better athlete.

You are born having inherited roughly half your DNA from your mom and half from your dad, leading to a unique combination that will make you, you. We can use that natural variation. By collecting the DNA of a bunch of athletes and non-athletes, we can figure out which gene variants are associated with being an athlete. This is called a Genome-wide association study. We use this method to learn about all sorts of traits – height, risk for heart disease and more.

This process is like trying to build the ultimate downhill bike park weapon bike by buying different components randomly from a bike shop, throwing them onto frames to build 'frankenbikes', and then doing timed laps to figure out which bike is best. You might say that bikes with downhill casing tyres are doing much better than the ones with light EXO casings. Tyre casing must be important for the trait of 'park-weaponness', and the downhill casing variant is associated with having fewer flats.

Analogously, ACTN3 protein is expressed in skeletal muscles, where it helps with the formation of the fast-twitch muscles that give sprint power. About 18% of people have a broken version of the ACTN3 gene, which does not make any protein. Elite power athletes are much less likely to have a broken version than the general population, so the functioning variant is associated with elite power athletes. [5]

But wait, EXO casing tyres aren't universally bad. If you were measuring your bike's at a cross country race, you'd be bummed hauling around downhill casings. Elite endurance athletes are more likely to have the broken version of ACTN3. Potentially, without this variant to form fast-twitch muscle fibres, they are left with *more* of the slow-twitch muscle fibres important in endurance.[5]

This has real implications for human health. For instance, most work on heart disease looks into what is wrong in people's hearts and then tries to come up with drugs to fix those problems. But a parallel approach is to look at what's going *right* with people with exceptionally good hearts – very high VO2 max – and try to make drugs to promote those things[6]. In this way, studying the genes of athletes can improve the lives and health of everyone, elite athletes or not.

"By collecting the DNA of a bunch of athletes and non-athletes, we can figure out which gene variants are associated with being an athlete"

1. Sarzynski, M. A. & Bouchard, C. World-class athletic performance and genetic endowment. *Nat. Metab.* 2(9), 796–798 (2020).

2. Bouchard, C. *et al.* Familial aggregation of VO(2max) response to exercise training: results from the HERITAGE Family Study. *J. Appl. Physiol. Bethesda Md 1985* 87(3), 1003–1008 (1999).

3. Moor, M. H. M. D. *et al.* Genome-wide linkage scan for athlete status in 700 British female DZ Twin Pairs. *Twin Res. Hum. Genet.* 10(6), 812–820 (2007).

4. Nezhad, F. Y. *et al.* Genes whose gain or loss-of-function increases endurance performance in mice: a systematic literature review. *Front. Physiol.* 10 (2019).

5. Yang, N. *et al.* ACTN3 genotype is associated with human elite athletic performance. *Am. J. Hum. Genet.* 73(3), 627–631 (2003).

6. Ashley, D. E. A. *The Genome Odyssey: Medical Mysteries and the Incredible Quest to Solve Them.* (Celadon Books, 2021).

SEBASTIAN SCHIECK

ROUND 1 MAYDENA AUSTRALIA

ENDURO WORLD CUP / ROUND 1
MAYDENA / AUSTRALIA / 26/03/2023
42.7553° S / 146.6283° E

Opposite: Ryan Gilchrist rode well all day, finishing in the top-ten on all but one stage and ending the race sixth overall.

SEBASTIAN SCHIECK

COOL TURNS & BIG FERNS

Words: James Lumley-Parkin

Are we there yet? Oh, this is it!

After the better part of two days travelling across the globe, the small town of Maydena may seem underwhelming and have you second-guessing if you're in the right place. Along a winding road to nowhere, nestled in a dense forest of Eucalyptus, this small, unassuming town has little to no sign that the best in the world will be racing the first-ever Enduro World Cup in a few days.

The town was once home to osmiridium miners, but the 1950s saw the logging industry move in. Fast forward to 2018, when Simon French and company finally came to an agreement with Forestry Tasmania to transform part of the forest into a bike park. French and his trail-building company Dirt Art evidently had a strong vision of what the place could become. They have quickly built over 80km of some of Australia's finest trails. With a plethora of trails winding its way down through the forest, the best

SVEN MARTIN

way to describe the local trail map is as if an unruly two-year-old threw a bowl of spaghetti against a wall, and most of it stuck.

The unobtrusive, retired primary school building has been converted into the bike park's base. Walk around the back, and you're met with the hubbub of the mountain bike circus. A bustling café, kids flying around the pump track and a constant stream of uplift vans stand in stark contrast to the seemingly sleepy town.

SEBASTIAN SCHIECK

The enduro World Cup took place in autumn, so the mornings were crisp, but the days pleasantly warm. Harsh winter conditions in the Northern Hemisphere seemed to have hampered some athletes' off-season training, so it was no surprise that the Australian locals would enjoy a home-turf advantage. The pro field looked stacked, with several gravity-fed racers joining the ranks. Notable downhillers included Valentina Höll, Connor Fearon, Troy Brosnan and the Meier-Smith brothers (Luke and Remy).

With the new season came a new race format – we'll get to that later – and some team reshuffles. The biggest switch was Jesse Melamed's departure from Rocky Mountain after 16 years, moving to Canyon. Slawomir Lukasik picked up his first factory deal with Yeti, and Jack Moir joined YT, with their return to enduro, alongside Kasper Woolley and Christian Textor.

Fortunately, Friday's practice was relatively uneventful. Some wet weather moved in later in the day, but the riders stayed protected from the high winds and rain by the thick tree canopy, and the trails seemed unscathed too.

A new addition for 2023 was a rest day between the practice and race days. The consensus was that this was a welcome change; it would give athletes time to rest and mechanics leeway to get the race rigs primed and ready for race day.

Breaking through the early morning mist, the first of two uplifts of the day deposited the riders at the very top to ride down a neutralized section of stage six to get to the start of the first stage of the day, 'GnarYeah' – four km in length with a chunky 720m of descent. The morning's moisture made some sections up top a little unpredictable, but quickly the trail dried out with more and more tyres churning up an already rutted track. This stage had many line choices (cheeky inside or high and wide?). Easy to remember for a few corners, but a little harder to navigate on a seven-minute-plus track with weary eyes.

From the get-go, local knowledge gave the Aussie riders an edge, and the rest of the field would be playing catch-up throughout the day. Of course, there are exceptions to the rule, with Richie Rude, Jesse Melamed and Rhys Verner managing to turn up the pressure. Tasmanian-born Dan Booker, who previously worked in Maydena as a trail builder, tore down the opening stage and landed his first World Cup stage win. Just over a second back was Giant Factory Off-Road's newest signing Luke Meier-Smith, with the steep stages suiting him. Rude came in third, with Melamed milliseconds behind. True to form, Isabeau Courdurier did what she does best and took the first stage of the year. Just over three seconds back, though, was Höll, letting Courdurier know that winning wouldn't be easy. Only two hundredths behind Höll was flat-pedalled Morgane Charre, looking confident over the rough terrain.

"IT'S THE BEGINNING OF AUTUMN HERE, THE DAYS ARE PLEASANTLY WARM"

At just under two km, 'Outer Limits' should be short and sweet, but with only 250m of descending, this was going to a physical stage. As its name suggests, the stage took racers to the eastern edge of the bike park, where the trees and ferns are densely packed. As this stage was hard to reach for spectators, it was an eerily quiet affair compared to the rest of the day. This stage would favour someone strong on the pedals who could carry consistent speed through the hard-packed turns. Melamed danced amongst the wooden giants to take the stage win, proving he had no problem getting to grips with his new setup. Luke Meier-Smith, leaning on his BMX background, pumped and powered his way to second, with Booker less than two seconds behind. This shorter stage also seemed to suit Höll, who put nearly three seconds into her competition. Bex Baraona had a heater of a run to come second in front of Ella Conolly.

After the quiet of stage two, in came the noise! This is what racing in Australia is all about. The Tassie crowds had already proven to be some of the rowdiest fans in 2017 and 2019. This year would be no exception. The 'Heckle Fest' was in full swing, carefully orchestrated to get the fans to the best spots on as many stages as possible while making the most noise possible. Along with a DJ blasting out tunes at the top of stage three, riders were treated to deafening chainsaws, air horns and many retired bike parts being smashed together. The riders matched the crowds' energy, putting on one heck of a show.

Melamed practically broke the internet with his near-death experience on the big step down. After a short gasp, the crowd erupted as he managed to save it, landing sideways but somehow riding through the next berm with his outside foot detached from his pedal. This wild run landed

Melamed in 70th place on the stage, seemingly dashing his chances of a podium spot. Spurred on by the home crowd, it was a 1-2-3 for Australia, with Luke Meier-Smith winning his first stage in the elite ranks. Ryan Gilchrist of the Yeti/Fox team got his best result of the day, coming in second, with Booker in third. Höll held her own as she took another stage win in front of Conolly and Charre. But with three more stages, it was anyone's game. It was incredibly close racing, with only eight seconds separating the top four women.

Stage four, 'The Natty', was the shortest but most brutal of the day. As Maydena's purpose-built downhill track, it was fast, rough and loose. This stage would be full-on, with bikes and riders refreshed after the tech zone. Brosnan smashed it and took the stage win, jumping up four places in the overall. Melamed made up for mistakes on stage three and took second in front of Booker. Courdurier was back in the fight and took the stage ahead of Charre and Conolly.

Stage five was a mishmash of six different trails crisscrossing down the hill, with a good mix of gnarly, steep tech and some flowy bike park to keep riders on their toes. Once again, the locals dominated, with Luke Meier-Smith out front, closely

SO THE MORNINGS ARE CRISP, BUT

followed by Booker and Fearon. Courdurier won again, slowly increasing her overall lead in front of Charre and Conolly.

The most significant change to the format for 2023 was the reseeding for the final stage at most races. After an uplift to the top, all that stood between the riders and the finish corral was 'Tech as Heck', a monster stage five km long with 820m of descending.

With incredibly tight times within each category, it was all to play for. However, Luke Meier-Smith managed to keep his cool and handled the pressure with gusto, taking the stage win by only two hundredths but cementing his victory nearly six seconds ahead of Booker. Fearon wrapped up a solid day in third after being in the top five in all but the first stage.

Charre managed to steal the last stage by a fraction of a second, but it wasn't enough to rob

Courdurier of her victory. Conolly lost precious time with a mechanical early on her final run but managed to hold on to third overall.

With the crowd's echoes slowly replaced by the evening chorus of cockatoos, it was time to pack up and head north for round two. If this first race was anything to go by, 2023 would be an absolute blast.

SVEN MARTIN

SVEN MARTIN

What a way to start the 2023 enduro season in beautiful surroundings at a new venue as the Enduro World Series changed name to the Enduro World Cup (EDR) for 2023 and beyond. Connor Fearon sliced through the Tasmanian bush on his way to third in the race.

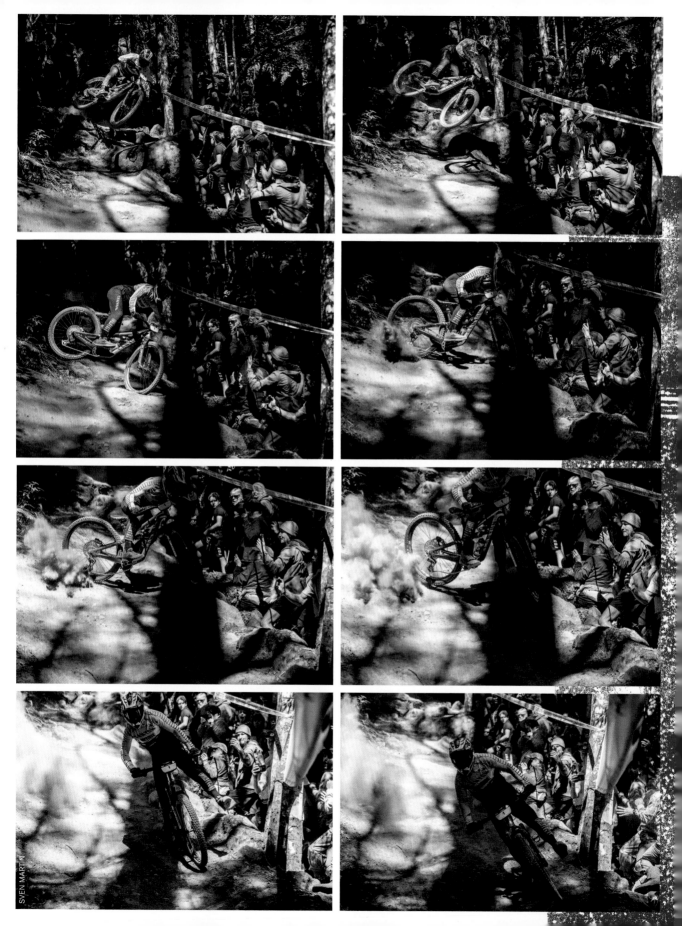

SVEN MARTIN

"TASSIE CROWDS HAD ALREADY PROVEN TO BE SOME OF THE ROWDIEST IN 2017 AND 2019. THIS YEAR WOULD BE NO EXCEPTION"

Opposite: Jesse Melamed's first outing on a new team started well with a win on stage two, but some hairy moments and a burped tyre saw him finish down the ranks in 19th at the end of the race. **Below:** Ella Conolly began 2022 with a first-round win; in 2023 she was back on the podium in third here in Maydena.

SEBASTIAN SCHIECK

SVEN MARTIN

SVEN MARTIN

Here: Despite a near-death moment where he came crashing across the finish line tangled in the metal course marking barriers, Alex Rudeau held it together for 12th in the race. Rudeau wasn't the only rider on flat pedals – in fact, two of the top-three men (Booker; Fearon) and one of the top-three women (Charre) were on flats too. **Above and opposite top:** Troy Brosnan was one of a raft of downhill pros who came out to race at round one. And it was no holiday – the likes of Brosnan and Vali Höll meant business. Fifth for Brosnan. **Opposite bottom:** Dan Booker scored his first-ever top-five at round one in 2022 and in 2023 he went even better, taking second in Maydena on trails he helped shape.

62

Luke Meier-Smith had raced enduros before in the Under-21 (U21) category (he dominated it in 2022), but Maydena was his first in elites. No fuss – the Aussie rode on the limit all day to take the win in this first-ever UCI-sanctioned Enduro World Cup.

SVEN MARTIN

SEBASTIAN SCHIECK

Above: Morgane Charre continued her form from 2022, winning the tough stage six and finishing second in the race. **Opposite:** Rhys Verner's season would go from strength to strength. Fourth here for Verner, his result helping Forbidden Synthesis win team of the day.

"A CHANGE TO THE FORMAT WAS RESEEDING FOR THE LAST STAGE"

SVEN MARTIN

Reigning champion Isabeau Courdurier put her stamp on the 2023 series, winning half of Maydena's stages and taking the race overall. With series points for every stage result in 2023, a consistent day in the saddle could pay dividends later in the season.

SVEN MARTIN

SEBASTIAN SCHIECK

SVEN MARTIN

This page: Morgane Charre (top), Isabeau Courdurier (middle) and Tasmania's very own Dan Booker (bottom) celebrate podium finishes. **Opposite:** The Giant Factory Off-Road Team had been reinvented for 2023 and at its first major showing the team went straight to the top, with Luke Meier-Smith winning his first elite-level Enduro World Cup.

SVEN MARTIN

SEBASTIAN SCHIECK

STAGE STATS:

STAGES	DISTANCE (KM)	DESCENT (M)
6	54.5	2511

TIME CHECK:

FINAL RACE RESULTS

Men		Women	
1. Luke Meier-Smith	28:55.21	1. Isabeau Courdurier	33:15.93
2. Daniel Booker	+5.83	2. Morgane Charre	+9.58
3. Connor Fearon	+19.24	3. Ella Conolly	+37.72
4. Rhys Verner	+24.57	4. Rebecca Baraona	+40.08
5. Troy Brosnan	+26.71	5. Harriet Harnden	+43.60

STAGE BY STAGE

STAGE 1

Men
1. Dan Booker	7:20.69
2. Luke Meier-Smith	+1.17
3. Jesse Melamed	+4.97

Race Leader: Booker

Women
1. Isabeau Courdurier	8:27.42
2. Valentina Höll	+3.43
3. Morgane Charre	+3.45

Race Leader: Courdurier

STAGE 2

Men
1. Jesse Melamed	3:45.48
2. Luke Meier-Smith	+0.97
3. Dan Booker	+2.30

Race Leader: Meier-Smith

Women
1. Valentina Höll	4:15.65
2. Rebecca Baraona	+2.96
3. Ella Conolly	+2.97

Race Leader: Courdurier

STAGE 3

Men
1. Luke Meier-Smith	2:03.44
2. Ryan Gilchrist	+2.96
3. Dan Booker	+2.99

Race Leader: Meier-Smith

Women
1. Valentina Höll	2:23.55
2. Ella Conolly	+2.28
3. Morgane Charre	+2.30

Race Leader: Höll

STAGE 4

Men
1. Troy Brosnan	1:28.12
2. Jesse Melamed	+0.99
3. Dan Booker	+2.56

Race Leader: Meier-Smith

Women
1. Isabeau Courdurier	1:46.69
2. Morgane Charre	+2.19
3. Ella Conolly	+2.93

Race Leader: Courdurier

STAGE 5

Men
1. Luke Meier-Smith	4:08.59
2. Dan Booker	+2.96
3. Connor Fearon	+3.97

Women
1. Isabeau Courdurier	4:46.06
2. Morgane Charre	+2.29
3. Ella Conolly	+5.77

STAGE 6

Men
1. Luke Meier-Smith	10:04.26
2. Dan Booker	+0.02
3. Connor Fearon	+1.12

Women
1. Morgane Charre	11:30.29
2. Isabeau Courdurier	+0.50
3. Rae Morrison	+9.15

Hype Pivot?

Words: Dan Roberts. Image: Sven Martin

With so much of an enduro bike's recent evolution coming from the world of downhill, it was only a matter of time before high-pivot suspension designs found their way into the little bike world. But is there an actual benefit to performance in enduro race bikes, or are brands riding the wave of high-pivot hype from the glory of World Cup wins?

High pivots aren't a new idea. Do your history homework; they've been around in one shape or another for probably longer than you've been riding bikes. But their resurgence since 2018 has been the most notable and had the biggest impact on the industry and shape of bikes.

Stand trackside at a downhill World Cup, and you'll see more Commencals under privateer racers than any other bike. It was the Andorran brand, with the help of racers like Myriam Nicole and Amaury Pierron, who linked high pivots with winning in so many people's minds.

But bikes are a complex balancing act of more ingredients than Mary Berry's latest cake recipe. While the marketing departments throw around phrases like bump-gobbling and magic carpet, high-pivot systems bring unique advantages and disadvantages to the enduro world.

Moving a bike's main pivot, real or virtual, high enough that you need to use an idler pulley is when you're officially in the high-pivot club. It's done for one main reason – a more rearwards axle path.

Travelling down the trail, your bike encounters impacts at the rear wheel that will want to move the wheel vertically but also push it back horizontally. As enduro race tracks get rougher, with some stages on downhill tracks, like at the final round in Châtel, bump absorption becomes ever more important.

High-pivot systems allow the rear wheel to move more aligned to this bump direction, better absorbing the impact, robbing you of less forward momentum and spreading the impact out over a longer duration, all leading to better stability and letting you be less affected by the bump you just hit.

But perhaps the first downside is the opposite of its greatest advantage – once your wheel has finished compressing, it needs to rebound back.

As the wheel comes back through its travel, it's now firing straight into the next impact at a worse angle, where it has to slow down, stop and accelerate again before it starts to absorb. In singular impacts, that rearwards axle path has a clear advantage. But as the impacts come thick and fast, that advantage dwindles.

Idler pulleys allow a high-pivot system to handle the sheer amount of chain length change as your wheel moves further away from the bottom bracket. But it also adds another level of tunability to the bike and characteristics like anti-squat. Some idlers even move as the suspension does, further increasing the level of tunability on offer. The link between anti-squat and pedal kickback also weakens with the addition of an idler.

While adding that idler is necessary, it also adds parts, complexity and weight to the bike. Idler pulleys are notoriously loud when poor drivetrain maintenance leaves them dryer than the Sahara, with added drag, too. There is also the potential for more wear, with brands now resorting to enormous pulleys and even steel to make them last. And with less wrap around your chainring, the chain can lose its hold with more ease when things get wild, necessitating further guides and guards.

Gone are the days of as short a chainstay as possible, and high-pivot bikes grow incredible chainstay lengths as they compress. While a longer chainstay can add stability to a bike, so much change so fast can mean you have to think about what the bike might do next, as the bike shape rapidly changes and the tyre load fluctuates front and back. While there are more things at play in how a bike rides than just if the high-pivot box is ticked, many tend to need a learned riding style rather than an intuitive one.

With more brands jumping on the high-pivot bandwagon for performance and marketing reasons, has there been a shift in the bikes gracing the podium?

While there has been a high-pivot bike on the podium at every round of the EDR, and in six out of twenty-eight cases at the top, they've never represented more than a third of the potential twelve bikes on the combined elite and U21 men's and women's podiums. The overall podium for elites was noticeably absent of high-pivots, whereas the Forbidden of Emmy Lan dominated and took the overall win in the U21 category alongside another high-pivot bike. Yet, in the U21 men's, a high-pivot never made it to the podium once.

What decides a good enduro race bike, or even the win, is far more than how high the pivot is. Enduro bike development is a game of give and take in many areas. As we see the latest generation of high-pivot bikes coming with perhaps more balance in all their factors than early iterations, will we see the dominance that high-pivots enjoyed in downhill racing? Only time will tell if it's high-pivot hype or the next step in enduro bike evolution.

"Moving a bike's main pivot, real or virtual, high enough that you need to use an idler pulley is when you're officially in the high-pivot club"

The Land Of Inconvenience

Words: Miranda Miller. Image: Sven Martin

Italy, to a crass North American like myself, is the ultimate Land of Inconvenience. This is, of course, one of its most charming traits, and you learn to love it. At the exact time you think you'd like to eat something, the shops are shut. You'd like to do something on a Sunday? Wait until Monday. You've parked your car in a free, long-term parking spot? Well, sometimes it's free, and sometimes it's long-term.

A week of filming, followed by racing the Finale Enduro World Cup, had proved intense. This episode of 'Here, There, Everywhere' had held, heading in, the most question marks. The story we filmed and the week we shared with the extraordinary people behind the riding scene there had been tiring but rewarding. I could mentally cross another project off the list and enjoy a few moments before focusing on the next, starting Monday. Rolling down the street, Graeme and I had our usual discussion: pizza or pasta?

This blissful feeling of satisfaction quickly turned into a rock sinking into the pit of my stomach. The street that had been lined with cars was now empty. Our trusty Renault: gone. It was 7pm on Saturday. First thing Monday, we were booked to fly from Nice to Helsinki. Our chances of a) finding the car and b) getting it back on a Sunday in Italy felt incredibly slim.

Panicked, I messaged our Airbnb host, who had assured us of parking security, and Riccardo, who had been helping with the week's filming. Experience has shown me that Italians will jump to help you – though they will never attempt to change the system causing the problem – and we soon had two options: call the mayor or track down a cousin's friend. As much as I wanted to call the mayor, I thought we should start with the cousin's friend.

Our apartment was part of a family compound. Within 15 minutes of my call, the gate flew open, and our host, Francesca, exploded forth, urging me to follow. Ahead of us, another door blew wide, and her father came running out, looking excited and clutching his car keys. Both yelling (or speaking nicely; I couldn't tell), they forced me into the front seat, no matter how much I tried to get in the back. There is something hilariously uncomfortable about being in the front seat of a stranger's car, let alone a foreign stranger. I sat, childlike, with my hands on my knees, unable to make small talk or even give directions, while Francesca leaned between the seats and cursed the local authorities with charming force.

Seizing the opportunity to show off his driving, her father squealed his small car into a dark

industrial park. For what felt like 20 minutes, we did laps. We hit dead ends and reversed at high speed. Then, we repeated the same route a few more times until, at last, we pulled up outside an intimidating wrought iron fence. The same fence I'd spotted flashing by about ten times already. Francesca told me to climb the fence to see if I could find the car. Clinging to the bars, I clicked the remote. The Renault flashed its lights at me from behind a large truck.

Success! The car was in the tow yard of the cousin's friend! Francesca, apparently satisfied, said, 'Now all we have to do is find the pizzeria!' What? I just stared at her, assuming it was a joke. But no. We were back in the car and off to find the pizzeria; I thought it was in the centre of town, but no – more laps of the industrial park. We used the same discovery method until we stopped outside what looked like an empty warehouse. A few lights shone from the third-floor windows, and a poster paper sign taped to the glass door read 'Pizza'. And at last, there he was: the cousin's friend, leaning from the window, yelling a greeting – either friendly or not.

We returned, and I paid the fee. I drove the Renault out of the work yard and found my way back, all the while wondering, 'Where the hell am I going to park?'

"We repeated the same route a few more
times until, at last, we pulled up outside an
intimidating wrought iron fence"

SEBASTIAN SCHIECK

ROUND 2
DERBY
AUSTRALIA

SVEN MARTIN

ENDURO WORLD CUP / ROUND 2
DERBY / AUSTRALIA / 01/04/2023
41.1478° S / 147.8011° E

Opposite: Jack Moir was on a new team for 2023 (YT Mob) but the season started off the back of a hand injury. Regardless, Moir was up to speed in Derby and took fourth in the race.

79

DIRT WARS: RETURN OF THE YETI

Round 2
Derby
Australia
01/04/2023

Words: James Lumley-Parkin

BORIS BEYER

Maydena sure did mix things up. The men's podium looked slightly different from what we'd grown accustomed to over the previous few seasons. Cages had been well and truly rattled, but riders and teams had a few days to regroup and reflect before round two. In the stacked women's field, racing was fiercely tight and gave us a glimpse of what could be a legendary season.

The drive up from Maydena to Derby showcased Tasmania's stunning landscapes. So often, you rock up to an event, practice and race, and before you know it, you're on a plane back home, having barely looked outside the race tape. But this time, there was plenty of time between rounds to enjoy the trip up north. Even the farmlands in Tasmania are pretty – endless rolling fields of golden grass baked in the glaring sun. But soon, we would be heading into the trees.

Once a bustling mining town with upwards of 3,000 inhabitants at its peak, Derby's population dwindled when the mines closed in the 1950s. It had one heck of a facelift in the eight years or so since the inception of the Blue Derby trail network. The exponential growth reignited the now-thriving town. Hailed as a role model worldwide, the town champions sustainable nature-based tourism as a more financially viable and necessary transition away from destructive industries like mining and logging.

Now, in its third outing on the world stage, seasoned riders knew what to expect with Derby – a stark contrast to the steeps of last week. Glen Jacobs and his World Trail crew have less vertical to play with in Derby than many other bike meccas. But what they lack in vert, they make up for in flow and an intrinsic understanding of how to reshape nature to get the best out of it. An added bonus is that the earth has the perfect composition for mountain biking: the holy grail of grippy granite, with the rocks sticking to rubber, even when wet, and the porous dirt draining efficiently to allow for all-season ripping.

Practice started on Thursday after a night of persistent heavy rain. The sound of the downpour on thin tin roofs all night was only matched by the crowd's roars the week before in Maydena. A handful of OGs were surely experiencing flashbacks of the

2017 race, one of the wettest in enduro's history. But for now, with the mist starting to clear in the valley, the clouds had dialled it back a notch to light drizzle.

It would be an all-pedal affair during the week. There were no uplifts in practice or race day, which was not bad, as moving would be key to staying warm. With good tree cover, sometimes it was hard to gauge how much it was raining – the only real indication was the consistency of the mud on the tyres. Little by little, things started to fall apart, especially when riders got to stage five, 'Cuddles', a brand-new trail. The fresh dirt was super soft and speed-sapping. Even with wet clothes, unusable goggles and grinding drivetrains crunching through the grit, most riders still enjoyed the experience, a testament to how good these trails ride, come rain or shine.

Planned or not, the new format, including a rest day after practice, turned essential. Mechanics had their work cut out, stripping bikes down to the bone and steadily rebuilding them. The one downside to granite is its destructive effects on bike parts once plastered. New brake pads, chains, cassettes and bearings were swapped to get the rigs back in shape

for race day. Bikes weren't the only thing being brought back to life. Photographers and video makers alike spent most of the day drying out wet camera gear in the hopes of being able to work on Saturday – race day.

On Saturday morning, a beautiful sunrise lit the low-lying fog, with patches of bright gold dazzling against the backdrop of the deep green ancient forest. Crossed fingers began to relax when it looked like the forecast would stay true, announcing a sunny day of racing. Through the crisp morning

BORIS BEYER

SEBASTIAN SCHIECK

"EVEN THE FARMLANDS HERE ARE OF GOLDEN GRASS BAKED IN THE GLARING SUN"

air, enthusiastic MCs ushered racers through the first-time check and then up the climb to the top of stage One.

'Roxanne', the first stage of six, was set to be a physically demanding stage with only 235m of descent stretched over three km of undulating singletrack, punctuated by rock features sprinkled throughout the stage. A technical but fast set of substantial drop-offs was in store at the first rock slab section, attracting media squids and spectators. The crowd put on one heck of a show for the riders, chainsaws revving and inflatable dinosaurs dancing. But this was a heckle zone at its heart, so sometimes riders would get the 'golf clap' or 'dog's barking'. Worst of all, the silent heckle, where riders would be wondering how deep they'd dug already, barely 30 seconds into the first stage, to cut out the screaming crowd completely.

The rest of the stage was a mixed bag of grippy rock and ever-evolving dirt. Some sections had the time and sunshine to start to dry, whereas other spots held on to the moisture making for some energy-sapping trails. These conditions favoured riders able to put out the big watts, like Richie Rude, who won the stage four seconds ahead of his teammate, Slawomir Lukasik, who finished ahead of Jesse

Melamed. Harriet Harnden, once again, leaning on her cross country skills, powered into first, narrowly ahead of Bex Baraona. Ella Conolly missed out on third by a fraction behind Aussie local and cross country aficionado Zoe Cuthbert.

Access to stage two was an idyllic pedal liaison around the Briseis Dam, with the trunks of ancient trees still standing bare, jutting out of the water. 'Dambusters' should have been named Lungbusters – another super flowy trail, but after the rain, it was a slog, forcing racers to sprint between the berms to keep momentum. Baraona and Harnden would be locked in battle all day, jostling for position at the front. Unfortunately, round one winner Isabeau Courdurier had a nasty crash at the end of practice, leaving her right calf painful and swollen. With gritted teeth, she pushed through the pain, somehow managing to hold on to fourth by the end of the day, focused on protecting her chances at the series overall.

'Trouty' and 'Detonate', icons in their own right, were next on the menu. Both trails have their fair share of gnarly features: Detonate with its infamous crack in the rock and Trouty with its exposed rock slabs and chunky gardens. The huge hunk of granite painted in the bright colours of a trout was a beacon

to eager fans, drawing them in close to the action. At the end of each stage, a sea of hastily discarded bikes lay ready to transport the droves of passionate onlookers to the next vantage point. The racing was turning out to be as electric as the crowds, with very tight times in both the women's and men's fields.

Yeti/Fox teammates Lukasik and Rude dominated Derby, collectively winning five of the six stages. After another close battle on the penultimate stage,

PRETTY - ENDLESS ROLLING FIELDS

BORIS BEYER

Cuddles, only four seconds separated them, with Rude ahead. The longest stage of the day was still to come, with a hefty climb back up to the top of 'Kamma-Gutza', voted trail of the year in 2019. Maybe Rude's extensive experience at the sharp end gave him the edge to beat his teammate again, winning the stage and taking home gold.

Lukasik managed to keep his cool under immense pressure, grabbing a third place on the stage and securing his first World Cup podium in second. Nobody else could match the speed and consistency of the Yeti boys. Jesse Melamed had a solid day, winning stage three, which set him up for third overall. Closely following were the familiar faces of Jack Moir, Martin Maes and Youn Deniaud, all stepping up after the downhill lads dominated the week before. Unfortunately, Luke Meier-Smith couldn't defend his leader's jersey after suffering from the flu the morning of the race. Later in the day, he scored two top-ten results but had to settle for 17th.

SEBASTIAN SCHIECK

Baraona and Harnden, much like Rude and Lukasik, had been fighting all day, seemingly in a category of their own. After more than 20 minutes of racing, a mere second separated them before dropping into the final stage! Baraona was calm and collected throughout. She was just out there enjoying riding her bike, she said. After a strong, consistent effort all day, Harnden suffered a crash, unfortunately, and, subsequently, a mechanical on the last stage. Baraona came out on top and added an Enduro World Cup win to her CV, cementing Yeti as the team to beat moving forward. With Harnden having to make do with second, Conolly grabbed the last spot on the box after a solid day on the pedals and one stage win under her belt.

The sun was setting on the beautiful Tasmanian outback and another rollercoaster of a race. The status quo, for now, seemed to be restored with familiar faces at the top. With two months before Finale Ligure, riders would have plenty of time to sharpen their bodies and minds, ready for the busy summer of racing ahead.

BORIS BEYER

Above: Derby's granite is perfectly grippy under tyre – and it'll tear your skin off if you get it wrong through this gap. **Opposite:** Awful conditions early in the week gave way to decent weather for race day, with the trails remaining damp and tacky. Perfect for cornering, not so good on Derby's long pedalling sections. **Opposite bottom:** Erice van Leuven giving it beans on her way to the U21 win.

SVEN MARTIN

Rémi Gauvin's day ended early after a harsh crash in stage one's savage rock garden. With less elevation than round one, Derby's stages required all the pumping, pedalling and carrying momentum possible, including staying off the brakes and charging hard through the technical sections. Sometimes flatter races can bite even harder than the steeper ones.

SVEN MARTIN

SVEN MARTIN

"THE EARTH HERE HAS THE PERFECT COMPOSITION FOR MOUNTAIN BIKING"

SVEN MARTIN

SEBASTIAN SCHIECK

Opposite: Round one U21 winner Sascha Kim carried his speed into the second race to make it two from two and hold the series lead going into the two-month break between Enduro World Cups. Kim had the privilege of riding in the new-for-2023 leader's jersey (seen in this photo). **Opposite top:** Morgane Charre signs one for the fans after finishing fifth in the race. **Above:** Sławomir Łukasik scored a career-best second place in Derby, just behind his teammate Richie Rude. **Here:** Legendary trail builder (whose World Trail company is behind Derby's mountain biking) Glen Jacobs with Dan Booker. Both wizards at shaping dirt.

SVEN MARTIN

SVEN MARTIN

Below: Derby's long, physical stages seemed to suit Harriet Harnden, who put in a strong ride to win two stages and finish second in the race overall. **Here:** You have to love mountain bike fans. **Opposite:** Dan Booker lives in Tasmania and is clearly comfortable with the terrain.

SVEN MARTIN

SEBASTIAN SCHIECK

Wow. Yeti-Fox were on a charge in Derby, with podiums a-plenty. Bex Baraona put her off-season training with the team to good use, powering home to her second career win. Gowaan!

SVEN MA

SEBASTIAN SCHIECK

SEBASTIAN SCHIECK

SEBASTIAN SCHIECK

Opposite: Richie Rude laid down some of his notorious power to take his first win of the season.
Opposite top: Bex Baraona's notes-to-self. **Top:** Łukasik, Baraona, Rude. 2, 1, 1. A brilliant team effort.
Here: Baraona's smile says it all.

"THE STATUS QUO, FOR NOW, SEEMED TO BE RESTORED WITH FAMILIAR FACES AT THE TOP"

STAGE STATS:

STAGES	DISTANCE (KM)	DESCENT (M)
6	42.5	1444

TIME CHECK:

FINAL RACE RESULTS

Men

1. Richie Rude	25:52.86
2. Slawomir Lukasik	+7.59
3. Jesse Melamed	+24.97
4. Jack Moir	+28.56
5. Martin Maes	+31.75

Women

1. Rebecca Baraona	29:52.01
2. Harriet Harnden	+8.22
3. Ella Conolly	+25.73
4. Isabeau Courdurier	+48.72
5. Morgane Charre	+49.85

STAGE BY STAGE

STAGE 1

Men

1. Richie Rude	5:16.17
2. Slawomir Lukasik	+3.98
3. Ed Masters	+5.99

Race Leader: Rude

Women

1. Hattie Harnden	6:12.18
2. Rebecca Baraona	+2.25
3. Zoe Cuthbert	+9.12

Race Leader: Harnden

STAGE 2

Men

1. Slawomir Lukasik	4:36.47
2. Richie Rude	+0.13
3. Jesse Melamed	+2.99

Race Leader: Rude

Women

1. Rebecca Baraona	5:10.68
2. Hattie Harnden	+5.11
3. Barbora Prudkova	+6.10

Race Leader: Baraona

STAGE 3

Men

1. Jesse Melamed	2:21.00
2. Dan Booker	+0.08
3. Bradley Harris	+1.37

Race Leader: Rude

Women

1. Ella Conolly	2:43.70
2. Hattie Harnden	+0.95
3. Gloria Scarsi	+2.22

Race Leader: Baraona

STAGE 4

Men

1. Slawomir Lukasik	3:49.34
2. Richie Rude	+0.38
3. Jack Moir	+1.98

Race Leader: Rude

Women

1. Rebecca Baraona	4:20.87
2. Hattie Harnden	+3.93
3. Morgane Charre	+5.97

Race Leader: Baraona

STAGE 5

Men

1. Richie Rude	3:11.56
2. Slawomir Lukasik	+0.37
3. Jesse Melamed	+0.98

Race Leader: Rude

Women

1. Hattie Harnden	3:38.69
2. Rebecca Baraona	+2.94
3. Leanna Curtis	+3.19

Race Leader: Baraona

STAGE 6

Men

1. Richie Rude	6:35.76
2. Jack Moir	+1.98
3. Slawomir Lukasik	+3.18

Women

1. Rebecca Baraona	7:38.00
2. Ella Conolly	+1.18
3. Hattie Harnden	+7.27

100

BORIS BEYER

ROUND 3
FINALE
OUTDOOR
REGION
ITALY

ENDURO WORLD CUP / ROUND 3
FINALE OUTDOOR REGION / ITALY / 03/06/2023
44.1689° N / 8.3416° E

Opposite: The Enduro World Series circus visited Finale every year in its decade of competition 2013–2022, either for EWS or Trophy of Nations events. For 2023, the race was just down the coast in neighbouring Pietra Ligure – familiar surroundings, fresh trails. Cole Lucas rode here in the 2020 EWS round and was back in the top-20 in 2023 on-board a not-quite-top-secret Ibis bike.

SVEN MARTIN

03/06/2023
/2023

SUNBURNT SUMMER HOLIDAYS

Round 3
Finale Outdoor Region
Italy
03/06/2023

SVEN MARTIN

Words: Morgane Charre

I'm sitting here in mid-October at home in France drinking a coffee, looking back over the results from Finale Outdoor Region, the third round of the 2023 Enduro World Cup. It's been a few weeks since finishing the season and autumn is in the air; we racers have been lucky as it's been a beautiful off-season so far. Now is a good time to reflect on the season after a much-needed short break.

Finale Ligure is one of the best-known mountain biking spots in Europe. It isn't a resort, no chairlifts, but there are literally hundreds of trails and it's truly developed for mountain biking, with shuttle buses, bike shops and rider-focused accommodation. You can get 'biker menus' in many local restaurants. Finale has every type of trail: easy, short; very hard, long. The town is on the coast, but you can quickly gain some altitude by either shuttling up to the famous ex-Nato Base or the Din restaurant – the two main drop-off points – or gearing up for a long two-hour pedal from the beach to around 1,000 metres' altitude.

BORIS BEYER

High up in the hills the terrain is earthy with tree roots, and as you descend towards the sea it gets rockier. In the mountains it's calm, just riders and a few shuttle buses; near the coast there's the bustle of people, the scream of Vespas and small three-wheeled motorised things. When you get to Finale's main square after a ride, you find everyone having an apero with spritzes and mini pizzas and lots of loud chats – the day's stories, two-wheeled adventures. There's a lot happening and much to do.

We got to Finale late May-early June after nearly a two-month break since the first two rounds of the World Cup. The results at those first rounds had been quite different to what we expected, and we were looking forward to seeing how the season would play out from here.

Points were super tight in the women's rankings and, surprisingly (as the reigning champion and someone we're used to seeing on top), Isabeau Courdurier wasn't leading the series coming into round three. Bex Baraona's season was off to a good start with a solid result at round one in Maydena and her second-ever Enduro World Series-Enduro World Cup victory at round two in Derby putting her atop the points table. In the men's, Richie Rude was leading the series after the first two rounds after a seventh-place finish at the first round and a win at the second one. Just behind him, Dan Booker and Luke Meier-Smith, the surprise round one winner, sat second and third in the rankings. Two of the favourites for the series, Jesse Melamed and Jack Moir, sat further back in the points in fifth and eighth.

Finale's been hosting enduro races since the very first year of Enduro World Series racing in 2013 and is usually the final event of the season, making it a party and wind down for everyone. Racers know Finale well from all these years of visiting – we all have our favourite cafés (Sbuccia in Finalborgo), restaurants, spots on the beach and so on. Everyone feels good here and many come back to train and test bikes during the winter. It's the home of enduro in Europe.

But for 2023 things were a bit different. Firstly, the race wasn't in Finale, it was just down the road in Pietra Ligure, a five-minute drive west along the coast. (We raced in Pietra during the 2020 Covid season but the 2021 EWS and 2022 Trophy of Nations events were back in Finale.) Also, as it was pretty much summer on the Italian Riviera, things were getting really hot, and the ground was baked hard

103

"IN THE MOUNTAINS IT'S CALM, JUST NEAR THE COAST THERE'S THE BUSTLE OF PEOPLE, THE SCREAM OF VESPAS"

BORIS BEYER

and dry for this first round in a block of three up-coming World Cups. A lot of racers were staying right on the beach so we could stroll to the sea for a quick refresher – admittedly, it felt like summer holidays.

After such a long break from racing, it was like the start of a second season. Especially in the women's where the points were so close that it was almost like starting from scratch. The two first races in Tasmania meant everyone could see where they were at – weak points, strengths – and adjust their training accordingly, work on things during the gap between rounds and get set for the quite different European rounds. For most of us, there hadn't been a great deal of racing between the World Cups – in France we'd had the National Championships but otherwise we had little to gauge our progress and the level of our competitors. We'd soon find out.

Race day began with a shuttle from coastal Pietra right up to the Din drop-off point – from bright sunshine leaving town up into the mountains where things looked a whole lot more menacing overhead. From there we pedalled up through the forest, away from the roads, climbing, descending, riding quite far from the shuttle and arriving just below Monte Carmo, the area's highest summit (1,389m). Stage

one was long, more than eight minutes for the fastest riders, and packed with corners, tight through the trees, a bit like a pumptrack in places where you had to really work to generate speed. There was also a decent climb in the stage; it was a physical one for sure. I had a good ride here to win the stage and I really enjoyed the trail – I love that sort of stuff. Rhys Verner seemed to have a good time too and he won the stage by three seconds.

There was a hard climb across to stage two, which started high in the hills. As we pedalled this longest liaison of the day, the weather was turning; at the start of the stage, a few drops of rain seemed ominous. The stage was long, quite similar in style to the first one but more natural and rougher. For the top racers, it was about nine minutes of fun and varied riding – fast up top, rocky sections and flat turns, then into steeper stuff near the end. I had another good ride here, winning the stage by a good margin – it was just one of those days when everything seems to work. Melamed took the men's win by five seconds. As they were so long, these first two stages were where the day could be decided; Melamed and I were leading in the race overall as we headed into the shorter stages.

After a short ride across to the start of stage three, our surroundings changed and we found ourselves in the coastal area – dusty, rocky, dry. The clouds had cleared and there was a bright blue sky overhead; it was scorching hot. Stage three was full of turns with no support, just dust and rubble to try and get some traction. You had to brake early and anticipate your turns – there was no flow to this trail. Raphaela Richter won by 2.5 seconds on this sub-three-minutes stage. Alex Rudeau put his flat pedals to use to win the stage and move up through the overall results.

The sun was beating down as we pedalled up an exposed 4x4 track; Finale is always a physical challenge, and this year was no different – especially with it being during the hotter months. In fact, it was

RIDERS AND A FEW SHUTTLE BUSES;

probably the hardest race of the year. Stage four was, well, tight, rocky, dusty, and in my opinion quite dangerous. You could go fast but it was sketchy – at any moment you could have a massive crash in this unpredictable terrain. Local hero Gloria Scarsi's aggressive style worked and she took the stage win, but the times were tight. Melamed always seems rapid on these sorts of trails – his technical skills come to use when it's tight and tricky. Melamed won the stage.

Lunch – one of Italy's favourite meals. We were happy to stop for a break at this point after a so-far long day in the saddle. Cool down, rehydrate, reenergise. Then back to work. From the beachside pit area up to a small but steep mountain just outside town, we climbed on a seriously hot road to the start of stage five. We were left to suffer solo on the uphill, but as we dropped into the stage there were lots of spectators – the last two stages of the day were more accessible than the earlier ones for fans. Five was again dusty, the first half steep and the rest a bit flatter. You could quickly mess things up as it was so slippery in the dust; a good run required attacking where possible but staying clean

and mistake free. Courdurier took her first stage win of the day on this one. Verner kept it Canadian with the stage win in the men's.

Next, another scorching climb to the final stage of the day, which was on the same mountain as stage five but down a different slope. Melamed and I were leading the race by decent margins; on this short last stage we just needed solid runs to ensure the wins. But with the trails here cutting so tight to many trees, things could quickly go wrong.

Crowds lined the track and there was a good atmosphere. With some punchy climbs, you had to be dynamic on the bike and, after a long and tiring day, do your best to stay focused, mind on the job. Richter took another stage win here; Youn Deniaud scored his first stage of the day. Melamed and I both took sixth on the stage – enough to win the race and our first World Cup victories of the season.

It had been a proper long day of enduro racing, a real challenge to stay hydrated and on the bike in the hot and dry conditions. Great fun stages, and a perfect ice cream to finish.

SVEN MARTIN

Gloria Scarsi used to race as a track cyclist (she won the Under-23 World Champs) before switching to enduro in 2019. She now calls Finale home and at round three she put together her best race yet, finishing second – much to the delight of the local fans and friends out to support her.

SVEN MARTIN

SVEN MARTIN

SVEN MARTIN

Opposite top and left: Tommaso Francardo managed a career-best seventh here – a giant leap from his previous best of 31st. At home in Italy, on an Italian bike (Ancillotti) with a host of Italian sponsors. **Left and below:** A consistent set of stages carried Dimitri Tordo to fourth place. **Right:** José Borges pumped through the day's undulations to finish 20th. **Opposite bottom:** Dan Booker scored 23rd here – not quite what he'd have hoped for, but he stayed in the top-five series rankings.

SEBASTIAN SCHIECK

Main and above: European riders can cruise over to Finale anytime in the off-season for some quality trails and Italian culture. For Kiwis and other internationals, it isn't so easy to spend time here. Regardless, Charles Murray has managed top results here, winning the Trophy of Nations team event in 2022 and taking fifth in the 2023 Enduro World Cup.

SEBASTIAN SCHIECK

Here: Raphaela Richter stepped up the pace in Italy and rode to fourth place in the race. **Opposite top:** After recording her worst result of the season (fourth) at round two, Isabeau Courdurier stepped back onto the podium here in third. **Opposite bottom and below:** Wow. Rhys Verner had clearly been hard at work in the break between races and came back stronger than ever to take second in the race.

SVEN MARTIN

SVEN MARTIN

BORIS BEYER

"THE GROUND WAS BAKED HARD AND DRY FOR THIS FIRST ROUND IN A BLOCK OF THREE WORLD CUPS"

SVEN MARTIN

SVEN MARTIN

Main and below: The 2022 series champion (as signified by his arm band and #1 plate) Jesse Melamed ducked and dived through Pietra's trees and tech – its six stages across 56km with over 2,000m climbing and 3,000m descending – to score his first win of the season and take the series lead heading into round four.

SVEN MARTIN

Destroyer. Alex Rudeau took his first podium of the year here in third place. Rudeau's season got on a roll with this result and he'd never look back, finishing in the top-three at every race from here until the end of the series.

SVEN MARTIN

"A GOOD RUN REQUIRED ATTACKING WHERE POSSIBLE BUT STAYING CLEAN AND MISTAKE FREE"

Opposite and below: This is what pure joy looks like. Morgane Charre had clearly put in the work in the two months since the Tasmanian rounds and she battled through the day's heat to take her first win of the season here in Pietra. After the podium celebration, riders, teams and fans headed to Finale's piazza to celebrate in classic style.

STAGE STATS:

STAGES	DISTANCE (KM)	DESCENT (M)
6	58	2900

TIME CHECK:

FINAL RACE RESULTS

Men

1. Jesse Melamed	28:40.04
2. Rhys Verner	+5.38
3. Alex Rudeau	+6.26
4. Dimitri Tordo	+13.8
5. Charles Murray	+21.44

Women

1. Morgane Charre	32:22.32
2. Gloria Scarsi	+13.67
3. Isabeau Courdurier	+16.76
4. Raphaela Richter	+26.88
5. Mélanie Pugin	+41.32

STAGE BY STAGE

STAGE 1

Men

1. Rhys Verner	8:21.17
2. Charles Murray	+3.28
3. Richie Rude	+5.78

Race Leader: Verner

Women

1. Morgane Charre	9:16.25
2. Gloria Scarsi	+7.27
3. Isabeau Courdurier	+10.48

Race Leader: Charre

STAGE 2

Men

1. Jesse Melamed	8:54.16
2. Dimitri Tordo	+5.62
3. Alex Rudeau	+6.15

Race Leader: Melamed

Women

1. Morgane Charre	10:06.47
2. Gloria Scarsi	+7.20
3. Isabeau Courdurier	+8.31

Race Leader: Charre

STAGE 3

Men

1. Alex Rudeau	2:13.38
2. Youn Deniaud	+1.04
3. Richie Rude	+1.99

Race Leader: Melamed

Women

1. Raphaela Richter	2:29.80
2. Rebecca Baraona	+2.95
3. Morgane Charre	+2.96

Race Leader: Charre

STAGE 4

Men

1. Jesse Melamed	2:14.15
2. Alex Rudeau	+1.56
3. Jack Moir	+3.78

Race Leader: Melamed

Women

1. Gloria Scarsi	2:36.13
2. Isabeau Courdurier	+0.99
3. Morgane Charre	+1.01

Race Leader: Charre

STAGE 5

Men

1. Rhys Verner	3:58.68
2. Jesse Melamed	+2.20
3. Richie Rude	+2.99

Race Leader: Melamed

Women

1. Isabeau Courdurier	4:33.35
2. Gloria Scarsi	+0.47
3. Morgane Charre	+1.20

Race Leader: Charre

STAGE 6

Men

1. Youn Deniaud	2:45.19
2. Alex Rudeau	+0.66
3. Charles Murray	+0.78

Women

1. Raphaela Richter	3:11.99
2. Isabeau Courdurier	+0.97
3. Rae Morrison	+1.96

A New Dawn?

Words: Francesco Gozio. Image: Sven Martin

What's happening in the world of mountain biking? World Cup racing is undeniably in flux, constantly evolving and reaching new heights. But where is it headed? And how is a place like the Finale Outdoor Region adapting to these changes?

I'm Francesco Gozio, and I had the privilege of being the race director for the World Cups in the Finale Outdoor Region in 2023. While I don't hold all the answers, I can share insights from this year's successes.

From my early days riding as a child, I was fortunate to turn my passion into a profession, working as a professional mountain bike guide for almost a decade. After spending considerable time in the Finale Outdoor Region, I wanted to contribute to events like the Enduro World Series (EWS) to give back to such a vibrant community. My early volunteering efforts gradually enabled me to collaborate with the organising committee and with notable figures like Riccardo Negro, Andrea Principato, Maria Luisa Surico, Enrico Guala and Sofia Scafuro, to name a few. Great relationships and friendships blossomed throughout the years from this experience.

Finale has been a core destination for the EWS – now the Enduro (EDR) World Cup – since the beginning. The concept of the EWS was born in Finale, and for the past decade, it has been a recurrent venue on the EWS-EDR World Cup calendar. This year, there were significant changes in the sport's development. To elevate the sport to the highest professional level, WBD Sports and the UCI brought all mountain bike disciplines under the same umbrella, and enduro and electric-enduro were finally granted World Cup status.

Being the spiritual home of the EWS-EDR, we couldn't pass up the opportunity to host the first EDR World Cup round in Europe and a Cross Country Marathon round. While it represented a massive challenge, we seized it without hesitation.

In 2022, after an incredible tenure, Riccardo Negro took a break from his role as race director. I had big shoes to fill in. Moreover, our team grappled with the challenge of orchestrating three World Cup-level events during a bustling national holiday weekend. It represented a monumental task, including four consecutive days of racing, hosting about 800 riders and preparing over 100km of race course. However, the fundamental structure of these events remained somewhat familiar.

Describing the intricacies of race management is no simple task. Immersing oneself in events of such a scale offers a unique perspective, shedding light on aspects often overlooked by spectators and riders. Every team member confronts challenges ranging from medical safety planning and course design to precise paddock placements, stakeholder interactions and much more. All these elements must synchronise perfectly to produce an outstanding event. This is further complicated when operating in a location rich in history but fraught with logistical challenges and a diverse community of fans, advocates and critics. Navigating such an environment in a role as pivotal as race director can be intimidating. However, with a dedicated team possessing clarity, vision and passion, it is possible to excel. And our results spoke for themselves – the event was a resounding success.

Our event also facilitated interactions with other venues. We engaged in fruitful exchanges with Morzine and Châtel in Haute Savoie, France, sharing views and recommendations. These events can be fertile grounds for growth and learning. That sentiment resonates with my journey – filled with steep learning curves.

I had the incredible opportunity to embark on this journey in 2020, and it has allowed me to travel, improve and hone my expertise to the point where I can now support other event organisers in my role as World Cup sports coordinator.

Reflecting on the season, it feels like we were conceptualising the first EDR World Cup in Finale just yesterday, yet preparations for the 2024 event are already underway. This season, we overcame many challenges, witnessed the birth of a vibrant event in the Finale Outdoor Region and experienced memorable racing moments. The sport's trajectory remains an enigma, but the future is promising, with EDR solidifying its place among World Cup disciplines and E-EDR influencing the interplay of sport and technology.

I can't predict the future, but I'm sure that Finale is just getting started.

"The concept of the EWS was born in Finale,
and for the past decade, it has been a recurrent
venue on the EWS-EDR World Cup calendar"

Undefined Limits

Words: Matthew Fairbrother. Image: James Vincent

With an urge for a new challenge during the off-season, my sights naturally turned to the Highland Trail 550. Nestled in the Scottish Highlands, this 550-mile route, known for its challenging terrain and unpredictable conditions, was created to break anyone who attempted it.

There was a lingering void inside of me that needed to be filled. Feeling like I'd never truly reached my capabilities, this would be an all-or-nothing endeavour to unravel their true depths.

Simultaneously, the nearing Enduro World Cup series took priority. The difference between enduro racing and ultra-endurance racing is vast. The two disciplines collide with no grazing ground in the middle. It's one or the other, but I embraced the challenge and the present moment. I turned my focus inwards, reinforcing to myself that I'd done everything I could, and if I hadn't, well, at this point, it was simply too late. Everything I could control was controlled by then, and everything that wasn't was pushed out of my mind. It was time to face the unknown.

From the start, the biggest challenge lay within me. The pace of ultra-endurance riding was a drastic change from the gravity riding I was accustomed to. Hell, I knew I'd pay for any unnecessary exertion later. However, my mind rapidly faded due to a deteriorating foot condition. From the start, my feet remained wet from countless river crossings and marshland. I took every opportunity of refuge to dry and talcum powder them in a plea to mitigate the discomfort.

Nearing the end of day one, a storm rolled in, and the wind halted me in my tracks. I slept four hours to wait it out. Tired, cold and drenched, I awoke and questioned my decision as to why I set out on this challenge in the first place. What was the point of it all if I wasn't enjoying myself? This moment proved to be the biggest test of mental fortitude I've encountered. But what kept me going? Well, the fear of being stranded in the wilderness.

The northernmost portion of the route presented the first crux; headwinds and wet ground added to the challenge. A gruelling 2km of pure peat bog lay ahead of me, and with every step forward, my feet got sucked in, requiring an extraordinary amount of effort to keep moving. I was rewarded with a 30km road section that provided a temporary respite. Nightfall brought a new set of challenges in the form of chunky singletrack, which, on any other day, would have been a blessing. Concern grew as I had a few close calls with deer as they were easily spooked and consistently jumped out on the trail before me. A two-hour roadside sleep gave me enough rest to charge ahead into the third day.

Day three brought a series of unrideable passes, up and down, forcing me to walk over 64km. My moods largely fluctuated. The lowest came when a mental low coincided with an unrideable descent and a downpour. I trekked further into the remote highlands of Scotland – progress slowed as I traversed endless peat bogs.

As darkness approached, an unexpected storm descended on the valley. Forward progress was seemingly impossible. Trapped between two passes, I had no option but to push forward, battling the cold and risking hypothermia. Survival mode kicked in, and I pushed forward, desperate to maintain warmth. Blood streamed from my nose, a physical release of tension. I communicated my deteriorating condition to my film team and progressed to a nearby mountain hut. Shivering uncontrollably, I swapped my drenched riding clothes for my remaining dry clothes and huddled for warmth. Delirious and unaware, I was oblivious to the rescue efforts that had been initiated. I awoke from a daze to shouts of my name. My film crew had taken full responsibility and trekked four hours into the mountains and launched the mountain rescue team. Thankfully, shelter and dry clothes gave my body the chance to recover.

Mother Nature's unpredictability highlighted the importance of being prepared. I realised how vulnerable I was in that situation and wasn't prepared for it. I witnessed the selflessness of those who went above and beyond to ensure my safety. This challenge was all about me and my fault. In the end, I only completed 65% of the route, but I've been left with a more valuable lesson than if it had gone to plan. The Highland Trail broke me, but that's what I was striving for. I've learnt my limit and, well, now it's time to push that limit.

"Feeling like I'd never truly reached my capabilities, this would be an all-or-nothing endeavour to unravel their true depths"

Every Second Counts: Time Travelling The World Enduro

Words: Ines Thoma. Image: Sebastian Schieck

Walking through the pits after the Enduro World Cup (EDR) and E-EDR overall podium ceremonies in Châtel had a bittersweet taste to it – a spirit of optimism and anticipation towards the well-earned off-season but also the uncertainty and fear of an unknown future for many riders. Looking at my friends', racing colleagues' and competitors' faces reminded me of the beginning of enduro. Ten years ago, at a beautiful beach in Punta Ala, Tuscany, everything was new, uncertain and wild. Back then, we also felt the excitement of uncertainty and change, filled with youthful optimism.

Being there from the beginning and still riding for the same bike brand, Canyon, makes me feel a bit old but also happy and proud. I would've never wanted to miss any part of this beautiful journey – ten years of travels around the globe and the joy, sweat and tears shared with amazing friends worldwide. We had wild times during those first few years, like the 8,000-metre climb during two training and race days on a tiny peninsula near Corral, Chile, or Crankzilla in Whistler at almost 40°c and with empty water stations, or the French monster races with over 10,000 metres of descending in two days.

Coming into the sport with a cross country background suited me well when endurance and fighting fatigue were key during those long days and full race weeks. The top speeds and overall performance levels were not as high as those in today's field. We were less professional, given our lack of experience within the teams, but it was tough racing. I am super thankful for

the possibility of discovering exotic places like Tasmania, Colombia or Argentina and iconic mountain biking destinations like Rotorua, Winter Park and Whistler. It was a good mixture of racing, travelling and photo trips. We made the most of it and made friends around the world.

With the years and the format changes from two to one-and-a-half and single-day events, the requirements for racers developed increasingly towards downhill skills, with precision, speed and the will to take risks in every second and corner of every race stage – every second counts. After many years as a solid top-five contender and having been honoured to join several podium-champagne-sprayed parties, I felt the time had come to add more personal challenges.

While Covid brought the world to a dark standstill, our daughter Romy brightened our lives. I never doubted that I would return to racing and decided to run my little programme, which gave me more flexibility than the professional factory team setup I was used to. This decision became vital in my return to racing, keeping the pressure low and the stoke high. It allowed me to try different formats, like my first e-bike race, the E-Tour de Mont Blanc in Verbier and the E-EWS in Crans-Montana, Switzerland, in 2022.

Those two races opened my eyes to a new discipline in our sport, which didn't exist in my racing mind before. They provided so much bike time, technical high-alpine riding and

huge days on the bike. I felt again that spirit of adventure, which I loved during the early days of the enduro era and which I'd begun to miss at the world enduro races.

Back to Châtel: as the race ended, I looked forward to the changing landscape of World Cup racing but also backwards to my first full E-Enduro season, also the first season of the E-EDR. Cramming the e-bike and classic enduro races into the same day and racing similar stages made for a rather downhill-oriented race, but it raised the profile of e-bikes even more.

Reducing the batteries from three to two per day made the race days a little less adventurous and different from the classic race than I had hoped, but I was still stoked to get a few extra stages per day. The atmosphere among the girls was superb, and we all loved-hated the 'Power Stage', where you win or lose in front of a big crowd. While a mistake in a downhill stage typically results in a slower speed or foot dab, a mistake here leads to the 'Walk of Shame' – when you push up your e-bike as fast as possible.

I am proud to have completed another full season and happy to sneak onto the third podium spot in the overall. Before the last stage of the day (and the season), I was sitting in fourth in the race and overall. I focussed and went all in, winning the stage, climbing to third and finishing third overall with the tightest margin ever. So, my realisation of this first-ever E-EDR season is that every second (still) counts.

"With the years and the format changes from two to one-and-a-half and single-day events, the requirements for racers developed increasingly towards downhill skills"

SVEN MARTIN

ROUND 4
LEOGANG
AUSTRIA

ENDURO WORLD CUP / ROUND 4
LEOGANG / AUSTRIA / 15/06/2023
47.4396° N / 12.7623° E

Opposite: Morgane Charre won the downhill World Championships in Leogang in 2012. In 2023, Enduro World Cup racing made its debut here and she finished third.

BORIS BEYER

15/08/202
/08/2023

MAKING UP TIME

Round 4
Leogang
Austria
15/06/2023

Round four sprung itself on the Austrian Alps, several months after the Tasmanian races and just a couple of weeks since Finale Outdoor Region's scorching race. Leogang would be no ordinary enduro: for the first time, the Enduro World Cup (formerly Enduro World Series) would run alongside downhill and cross country in a triple-header event pitched as a sort of festival of top-tier mountain biking.

Grouping the disciplines would serve several purposes – such as streamlining the new World Cup organiser's massive organisational process, bringing the races to a large spectator base and uniting the diverse world of mountain biking in one place. It all sounded great in theory, but how would it play out?

Words: James McKnight

SVEN MARTIN

You will likely get different answers to the above question depending on who you ask and when. The truth is (according to us) Leogang was a rollercoaster of emotions for the enduro crowd. Yes, it was fantastic to be in a new venue, but the area has strict rules on where one can and cannot ride – it seemed this might limit the scope of the trails. Yes, being at a downhill and cross country World Cup could introduce a lot of spectators to enduro, but the race was on a Thursday when everyone was at work. Yes, it was cool to race alongside friends and teams from the other disciplines, but the enduro pits were sandwiched between a cycle path and some camper vans several kilometres from the race hub.

Racers were apprehensive before the race, and their worries only seemed to snowball as they arrived in Leogang to find their pits down the valley and their schedule strung out. It seemed like a neat idea to have the last of the planned six race stages run on the old World Cup downhill course, bringing enduro home to a roaring welcome by the amassed spectators in the finish area bowl. But reality looked like this: hours-long liaisons between stages and other dilly-dallying, waiting for the downhill track to free up after practice and junior qualifying. Stage six was pencilled for 8pm – sometime around sunset.

Due to everything mentioned above, the early week vibe was somewhat glum and even quite moany (sorry to say it), but things were on the up as soon as riders got on track and realised that they needn't have worried quite so much. The race would take in trails across Leogang and nearby Saalbach, a linked-up resort on the other side of the mountain (two of Austria's most famous bike park destinations) and comprise a range of terrain. Stages one to three were in Saalbach, with four to six in Leogang; on both sides of the hill, there were varying trails with rootsy tech portions, high-speed whacker-plated bits and some lung-busting pedalling. During the single practice day, there were still some reservations about the terrain and the course marking (some eccentric diversions off the main line of some tracks into grassy turns). Still, when it came to racing the following day, riders were pretty unanimous in praising the trails.

With the first three rounds' points tallies totted up, Jesse Melamed led the series rankings coming into

SVEN MARTIN

Leogang; in the women's, Isabeau Courdurier and Morgane Charre were level-pegging with 1,231 points each (Charre would wear the leader's jersey as she had most recently won an event). It wouldn't be the only time Courdurier and Charre would tie during a season of head-to-head battles.

The sun shone down as riders left Leogang's start-finish area early on Thursday, 15 June, to head out searching for gold. Two gondolas dropped them high in the hills, from where they began a taxing two-hour transfer to stage one. They had three hours to make it to Saalbach for the stage start, so most riders had an hour of hanging about, wondering how their day would pan out.

Ploughing into a short first race run on high-speed, hardpacked berms and rim-smashing rock gardens, the race finally woke up after a drowsy first few hours. Spectators were few, but a small number clung to the steep slopes where riders skipped and skewed through the last machine-built stretch to the finish line. Gloria Scarsi and Rhys Verner got off to a flying start with stage wins in elite women and men.

The day's highlight was up next. Stage two went into terrain enduro racers are more familiar with: raw, technical and long, with brutal rocks, tight turns in the exposed sections, and endless tree roots under tyre elsewhere. Experience paid off here, and Isabeau Courdurier and Richie Rude won the stage.

Transferring over to the other side of the valley, riders took a lift to the top of stage three, another

"LEOGANG WOULD BE NO ORDINARY THE RACE WOULD RUN ALONGSIDE DOWNHILL AND CROSS COUNTRY"

BORIS BEYER

SVEN MARTIN

Scarsi took another win on three, but Courdurier led the race overall at this point in the day, with Scarsi chasing in second and Morgane Charre in third. In the men's, Jesse Melamed recouped from a small crash earlier in the day to take his first stage win, but Verner was just behind – his strong ride putting him firmly in the overall race lead with Richie Rude in second and Alex Rudeau third. Riders transferred back to Leogang after a quick break at the mid-race tech and feed zone.

Stage four was a return to short, fast blasts at less than half the time of the preceding stage. It was smoother and faster than three but lung-busting nonetheless, with some full-on sprints. Raphaela Richter took her chance to jump into the ring here, winning the stage and putting her name into a growing list of contenders for the overall victory. It was a different story in the men's, with Verner keeping it consistent and taking the stage win.

Time was ticking, and the day was nearly done – but the race wasn't. By this point, racers had already been on the hill for some seven hours. As they dropped into stage five – a mix of roots and full-on pedalling – at around six in the evening, the clock had already run past the time they would have usually wrapped up racing, done podium celebrations and had an ice cream. Leogang brought a new endurance element to enduro. Courdurier and Rudeau took the stage wins on five before everyone cruised back to the pits for a lengthy break in racing.

As the evening light hit Leogang's craggy peaks, the enduro gang finally made their way up to a start gate somewhere in the lower reaches of the classic downhill course, just above all those turns Aaron

beast that was essentially a downhill race track only much longer – over 700 metres of descending across four kilometres. That meant big hits, fast turns and flat-out pedalling. Dust filled the valley floor and onlookers' lungs as rider after rider ripped around the last few corners at full chat despite having just put in an eight-minute effort.

Diving into the cool and calm riverside shade at the exit of stage three, racers could reflect on a savage stage and a so-far lengthy first half of the day.

ENDURO: FOR THE FIRST TIME,

Gwin famously railed with no tyre while leading the World Cup series in 2014. Now it was enduro's time to shine on Leogang's storied slopes. Stage six would be a short blast back into the start-finish arena riders had left nine hours earlier. While there weren't many spectators, it was cool to see lots of top downhillers hanging about long after their riding sessions to cheer home the enduro specialists. There's much respect between disciplines.

Courdurier, Scarsi and Charre held the top spots in that order as they dropped into the final stage. Men's series leader Melamed had hit further problems on stage five, dropping a chain and limping it home, the day's woes sending him plummeting through the overall results. That left the door open, and Verner, still going well and staying consistent, led the charge ahead of Rude and Rudeau in the race overall.

At barely a minute in length for the top men and scarcely more for the women, the final run into the finish was unlikely to shake things up dramatically in the standings. But with the sun now almost set (it was after eight before the top riders hit the track), bodies and brains tired from a long day in the sun, there was a chance it could still go wrong for those at the front of the pack.

Charre charged to the win on the final stage, making it a flashback to her 2012 downhill World Championships victory on this very course. The result gave her third place in the race overall, with Scarsi taking second and Courdurier earning a well-deserved win after a long day at the office.

You'd forgive Verner for taking a cruiser on this last stage – he was staring at his first-ever World Cup win, after all – but he was on a roll and went all-in to win the stage and the race in style – a massive result for the Canadian and one celebrated by his friends, supporters, compatriots and competitors alike. Rude and Rudeau rounded out the day's podium in second and third, respectively, just two and eight seconds behind Verner after 25 minutes of racing.

No matter the venue, conditions or circumstances, enduro always thrills. Love it.

SVEN MARTIN

BORIS BEYER

This page: Another week, another bike for Harriet Harnden, who raced the Lenzerheide downhill World Cup (finishing ninth) before heading to Leogang to race the enduro (fifth).
Opposite top: Jesse Melamed was leading the series coming into Leogang and he won a stage but his day was marred by a mechanical and a small crash. **Opposite bottom:** Dimitri Tordo was stylish as ever despite suffering from a crash in practice. He finished 20th in the race – a solid but disappointing result after his top-five at round three.

BORIS BEYER

BORIS BEYER

BORIS BEYER

Richie Rude was on the hunt all day, racking up consistent results and winning a stage to eventually finish the race in second, just two seconds behind Rhys Verner. Rude left Leogang wearing the series leader's jersey.

BORIS BEYER

"ROOTSY TECH PORTIONS, HIGH-SPEED WHACKER-PLATED BITS AND LUNG-BUSTING PEDALLING"

BORIS BEYER

Opposite and above: Gloria Scarsi has adapted her skills and rocketed through the results in just a few years on the World Cup circuit. Here she equalled her career-best result, finishing second. **Below:** Emmy Lan dominated the U21 category throughout 2023, including a win of over 17 seconds here in Leogang.

SVEN MARTIN

SVEN MARTIN

SVEN MARTIN

Above: The 2021 series champion Jack Moir's year just wasn't going his way. Moir rode practice but fell ill and missed the race. **Opposite:** With the enduro season split into three blocks of racing months apart, riders had long breaks to adapt their form. Charles Murray had a good run in block two, finishing top-five at each race, including fourth in Leogang.
Below: Morgane Charre (pictured) and Isabeau Courdurier were equal on points after round three, but Charre wore the series leader's jersey as she'd most recently won a race. Charre had another consistent ride here, finishing third.

BORIS BEYER

BORIS BEYER

Above: Raphaëla Richter had a solid outing in Austria, taking a stage win and fourth in the race overall. **Opposite:** Alex Rudeau's move from bicycle trials to enduro has paid off – in just five seasons of racing, he has become one of the riders to beat on the world circuit. Rudeau's 2023 season was well up to speed in Leogang, where he finished third.

BORIS BEYER

"YOU'D FORGIVE VERNER FOR TAKING A CRUISER ON THE LAST STAGE BUT HE WAS ON A ROLL"

Opposite and below: Rhys Verner's 2023 started with a top-five at round one, then he finished second at round three, and continuing the upward trajectory he went better still in Leogang, taking his first-ever elite-level Enduro World Cup win. Verner was never outside the top-five all day and won half of the stages.

BORIS BEYER

Isabeau Courdurier never fails to impress, managing top results seemingly in any conditions and circumstances. While some riders got tangled in the politics of an up and down week of schedule changes and limited communications from the race organiser, Courdurier kept her eyes on the prize and rode to victory.

SVEN MARTIN

STAGE STATS:

STAGES	DISTANCE (KM)	DESCENT (M)
6	71	4695

TIME CHECK:

FINAL RACE RESULTS

Men

1. Rhys Verner	25:08.74
2. Richie Rude	+2.77
3. Alex Rudeau	+8.72
4. Charles Murray	+22.41
5. Dan Booker	+28.87

Women

1. Isabeau Courdurier	28:35.01
2. Gloria Scarsi	+14.35
3. Morgane Charre	+18.56
4. Raphaela Richter	+32.16
5. Hattie Harnden	+34.20

STAGE BY STAGE

STAGE 1

Men

1. Rhys Verner	3:14.99
2. Slawomir Lukasik	+1.94
3. Alex Rudeau	+1.98

Race Leader: Verner

Women

1. Gloria Scarsi	3:37.48
2. Morgane Charre	+2.99
3. Raphaela Richter	+3.99

Race Leader: Scarsi

STAGE 2

Men

1. Richie Rude	5:24.38
2. Rhys Verner	+5.54
3. Alex Rudeau	+6.42

Race Leader: Rude

Women

1. Isabeau Courdurier	6:13.40
2. Gloria Scarsi	+11.02
3. Morgane Charre	+20

Race Leader: Courdurier

STAGE 3

Men

1. Jesse Melamed	7:44.17
2. Rhys Verner	+1.22
3. Richie Rude	+4.75

Race Leader: Verner

Women

1. Gloria Scarsi	8:41.08
2. Morgane Charre	+0.37
3. Isabeau Courdurier	+1.46

Race Leader: Courdurier

STAGE 4

Men

1. Rhys Verner	3:35.58
2. Slawomir Lukasik	+1.96
3. Alex Rudeau	+2.32

Race Leader: Verner

Women

1. Raphaela Richter	4:04.77
2. Isabeau Courdurier	+0.95
3. Morgane Charre	+1.18

Race Leader: Courdurier

STAGE 5

Men

1. Alex Rudeau	3:47.32
2. Richie Rude	+0.50
3. Charles Murray	+1.04

Race Leader: Verner

Women

1. Isabeau Courdurier	4:22.78
2. Hattie Harnden	+4.21
3. Morgane Charre	+5.09

Race Leader: Courdurier

STAGE 6

Men

1. Rhys Verner	1:11.41
2. Slawomir Lukasik	+0.97
3. Richie Rude	+0.98

Women

1. Morgane Charre	1:24.54
2. Raphaela Richter	+1.20
3. Mélanie Pugin	+2.28

ROUND 5
VAL DI FASSA
ITALY

Most riders refer to the Val di Fassa round as Canazei – because that's the town that hosts the race (the broader VDF area has eight lifts and 18 official mountain bike trails). Round five had five race stages that had all been raced in previous years, but riders were happy to be back in the Italian Dolomites racing on long, physical, varied tracks.

ENDURO WORLD CUP / ROUND 5
VAL DI FASSA / ITALY / 25/06/2023
46.4768° N / 11.7704° E

SEBASTIAN SCHECK

25/06/202
08/2023

TUTTI FRUTTI TECH

Round 5:
Val Di Fassa
Italy
25/06/2023

Words: Matthew Fairbrother

Rugged beauty flares through a heavenly green paradise – the lakes are its essence, the trails its veins. The mystic peaks of The Pale Mountains cast a shadow on the valley below, alluding to a dark past, although here they brew magic. The spirit of Dolomiti created the ultimate enduro mountain biking battlefield, a true catalyst for a fairy tale ending.

After the triple-header week of racing in Leogang, riders turned their sights to the Dolomites. Soaring from a vibrant, evergreen valley in Northern Italy, the mountains quickly evolve, and jagged-teeth-like rocks emerge. It's hard to arrive here without a sore neck. The views will keep your head turning in every direction. An almost casual turnaround from the last race meant teams rolled in at their own pace, slowly taking over the recluse town of Canazei.

KIKE ABELLEIRA

SEBASTIAN SCHECK

KIKE ABELLEIRA

You'll find this location on almost any mountain biker's bucket list. A true assortment of flavours to cater to everyone's trail tastes – luscious loam and chairlifts on one side of the valley, bike park tracks and raw trails on the other, all leading down to the gelateria at the bottom of the hill. Italians know how to do it right.

The riding on Canazei's doorstep is characterised by long, hard days in the saddle while at altitude. Being the fifth round of the UCI Enduro World Cup (EDR) and the last race of a full month of racing, there would be no hiding. This is as pure as enduro gets. Becoming a regular on the circuit, it appeared that this year's race would be a repeat of last year's, although that was far from the truth. Significant improvements had been made, and the trails were running all time. Rain was in the forecast – lots of it – and racers were in for a gruelling 44 kilometres and a burly nearly 3,000 metres of descending, which would put the racers to the test. The ascent would be assisted by the many ski gondolas in the area, although this shouldn't be overestimated. Racers still had to tackle half of the course by pedal power.

Richie Rude and Isabeau Courdurier won here in 2022, and with wins already under their belt in 2023, both were favourites for the weekend. Eddie Masters has a history of strong results in Canazei but wouldn't make it to the start line due to a shoulder injury. He'd be turning to team-mates Morgane Charre and Matt Walker to hold up the fort for Pivot Factory Racing.

Title hopes were forming with the season creeping over the mid-way mark, but with small margins, runners-up were ready to pounce for glory. In the men's, Rude had a substantial lead over Canadians Rhys Verner and Jesse Melamed. Verner was having his best season, including the previous weekend's win.

He'd be leaving it all out there. Alex Rudeau had also been consistently landing on the podium and was itching to climb the ranks.

In the women's, Frenchies Courdurier and Charre were in a season-long battle, with Courdurier holding the lead and Charre ready to capitalise on any of Courdurier's mistakes. Brits Bex Baraona and Harriet Harnden were waging their own contest, and the hunt for third was beginning to get heated.

The rain held off, leading to near-perfect conditions on stage one (Titans). The race began with a rude awakening for racers as they slalomed down ski pistes into fast, tight and awkward technical trails through the woods. Courdurier began as she intended to continue. She won the stage by almost six seconds ahead of Charre. Mélanie Pugin managed to find her feet again and finished an additional two seconds back.

The French had truly asserted their dominance in the women's field, but they weren't done yet as Rudeau stormed into first, two seconds ahead of Rude, in the men's. Verner rounded out the top three. After eight minutes of racing for the women and seven minutes for the men, it was still all to play for.

As racers made their way up to stage two, the sun had come out in full effect, reassuring them that the dust was here to stay. 'Infinity' was a fast blast through the alpine up top, passing through bike park berms before getting into raw, rooty and rocky singletrack right down to the bottom. Oh, and why not throw a one-and-a-half-minute climb mid-stage? As if it wasn't already hard enough.

"LOAM AND CHAIRLIFTS ON ONE SIDE OF RAW TRAILS ON THE OTHER, ALL LEADING KNOW HOW TO DO IT RIGHT"

SEBASTIAN SCHIECK

The French were unstoppable and were waging their battles out front. Courdurier secured yet another stage, with Pugin in second. Gloria Scarsi jumped into the mix with third place on the stage. Courdurier would hold on to the race lead only seven seconds ahead of Charre. In the men's field, Melamed proved to be a crowd-pleaser as he launched himself down the hill in true Melamed fashion, although his aggression would be one-upped by Rudeau, who edged him out by almost a second. Rude would round out the top three and hold on to the race lead ten seconds ahead of Melamed, but his day would go downhill.

Pained faces would be the theme of the weekend. Harnden used her cross country background and capitalised on it to become the first non-French stage winner of the day by ten seconds. Charre proved flat pedals weren't holding her back on the brutal climb as she charged her way into second. Chloe Taylor rounded out the top three with her best stage result. In the men's, Walker stomped his way into third, seemingly glued to Melamed's rear wheel, who slotted his way into second just ahead of him. Rude's trademark style of pure aggression paid dividends as he paved his path into first by six seconds. Courdurier and Rude were leading the race with three stages to go.

A pedal up the road brought racers to stage three (Electric Line), which they referred to over the weekend as 'the downhill stage.' With eye-watering fast straightaways, flat 90-degree corners, boardwalks and rock gardens, it had it all. Stage three was going to be an all-out affair. There'd be no letting off.

A pedal, a gondola, a hike and a load of fatigue would get riders to one of the most renowned enduro stages, Tutti Frutti. Despite its sweet-sounding name, this was one of the hardest stages on the circuit, with an exposed ridgeline, high-altitude sprints, rough corners, risky line choices and a dousing of loam to keep everybody from grimacing. Over five and a half kilometres and almost 1,000 vertical metres of descent (more than 12 minutes for the women and nearly 11 for the men). Once again, French domination continued in the women's field as Charre, Pugin and Courdurier went 1-2-3 in that order. In the men's, things quickly came unstuck for Rude, who suffered a flat tyre in the lower third of the stage. He did what he could to salvage his result and only lost about 25 seconds. Walker saw an opportunity and leapt. He'd been consistently in the top five all day but had finally made the move to take the stage win. Charlie Murray followed up behind four seconds back, making a Kiwi 1-2. Verner found his feet again after a rough couple of stages and landed nine seconds back from Walker.

THE VALLEY, BIKE PARK TRACKS AND DOWN TO THE GELATERIA. ITALIANS

With Charre scrapping ahead of Courdurier to go first and Walker capitalising on moving ahead three places into first, it was all down to the last stage. The pot was boiling. Ciasates was the shortest stage of the day but probably the most action-packed. At just over one kilometre long and with only 200 metres of descending, it would be an all-out sprint to the finish. Courdurier took the top step, with Pugin in tow and Scarsi following in third, once more, after a consistent day of riding.

Courdurier claimed another win in the women's, adding to the season's tally. Charre took a commendable second place after a smart day of riding, and Pugin found some form after a rough start to the season to finish in third. The new reseeding format built much tension in the men's race. Rude, Melamed and Murray fought for third with only two seconds separating them. Rudeau was sitting pretty in second, and Walker was on his way to picking up his first victory. Although no one was guaranteed anything, with such a short stage, one mistake would cost everything. Rude ploughed his way into third, edging out Murray and Melamed and lessening the blow to his puncture earlier in the day. Rudeau crossed the line into second after a standout season for the French national champ. Crossing the line in first place was Walker, who claimed his first elite win and the most popular win in recent enduro history.

Just like that, it was all over. Another superb weekend of bike racing confirmed to racers and spectators why we keep returning to this venue. Was it the views, the tracks, the pizza or the gelateria in town? It is hard to say.

Rude and Courdurier earned commanding leads in the overall title hunt, but it was far from over. Just below them, it was all up for grabs. With a two-month break from racing, the fires would be reignited, and racers would be charging as the circuit headed to the French Pyrenees.

KIKE ABELLEIRA

SEBASTIAN SCHIECK

ENDURO WORLD CUP / ROUND 5
VAL DI FASSA / ITALY / 25/06/2023

Opposite top: Alex Rudeau was on a roll and in Val di Fassa he made it three podiums in a row, finishing second. **Above left to right:** Matteo Nati; Andy Lund, Dan Booker and Kelan Grant. **Below:** In its five editions, the Val di Fassa race has become something of legend for its backdrops and epic stages. Tutti Frutti is one of the most demanding stages of the season. **Opposite bottom:** By this point in the season, the series was clearly going Emmy Lan's way. Here she made it three wins in a row and continued her charge towards a title.

Is this scene for real? Of course it is. That's the beauty of photography – you can be technically the best, the most devoted to your artform, have all the latest equipment. But a little magic and good timing (planned, of course) makes for the most memorable shots. Gloria Scarsi kept her focus and rode to fourth in the race.

"IT'S HARD TO ARRIVE HERE WITHOUT A SORE NECK. THE VIEWS WILL KEEP YOUR HEAD TURNING IN EVERY DIRECTION"

SEBASTIÁN SCHIECK

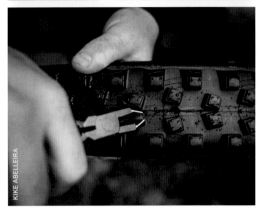

KIKE ABELLEIRA

Opposite: After a tricky 2022 season, 2021 series champion Mélanie Pugin's stars finally aligned and she stepped onto the podium in third. **This page top:** Pivot's Eddie Masters (on the computer in this shot) crashed out hard at round three and smashed up his shoulder – the first of two big injuries in 2023. But Masters never sat still, and he was trackside filming the action for his Ed Bull Media House video productions, as well as supporting his team-mates on their way to podium results. **Below:** Dan Booker (right) didn't have the answers for Jesse Melamed (left).

KIKE ABELLEIRA

Below: Rae Morrison has been a staple of the international enduro scene since her first Enduro World Series race in 2014 – she's raced in every series since. **Opposite:** Jack Moir was back racing after missing round three through illness, and the tall Aussie put in a solid ride for ninth. **Bottom:** Jesse Melamed said he struggled with arm pump on the longer stages in Val di Fassa. Still, he ended up fifth in the race – not a bad result by anyone's standards.

KIKE ABELLEIRA

KIKE ABELLEIRA

SEEBASTIAN SCHIECK

SEBASTIAN SCHIECK

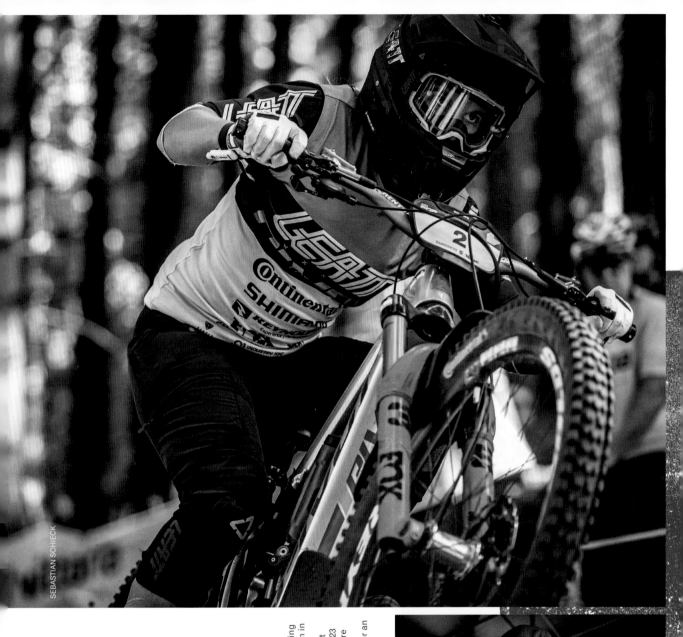

SEBASTIAN SCHIECK

KIKE ABELLEIRA

Opposite top: Lisandru Bertini's season was starting to take shape at this point. He took the Under-21 win in Val di Fassa, the second in a hat-trick of victories. **Above and right:** Morgane Charre put together yet another top result here, finishing in second. The 2023 title chase was really a head-to-head between Charre and Isabeau Courdurier. **Opposite bottom:** After battling to come back from a serious concussion for an entire year, it was great to see Estelle Charles back racing during the second block of World Cups.

"ANOTHER SUPERB WEEKEND OF BIKE RACING CONFIRMED TO RACERS AND SPECTATORS WHY WE KEEP RETURNING TO THIS VENUE"

Opposite: We've said it before and we'll say it again – no matter the conditions, circumstances, country, Isabeau Courdurier is always there or thereabouts (there, usually). Courdurier racked up another race win here, her third of the season so far. **Top:** Mélanie Pugin, Morgane Charre and Courdurier made it an all-French top-three.
Here: Noga Korem faced sponsorship struggles in 2023, moving to a Commencal bike after leaving GT during the break between blocks one and two of racing. She kept her composure and put in some solid results, including seventh in Val di Fassa.

Coming into the final stage, Matt Walker was leading the race and staring at his first-ever World Cup win. At this point he could have – perhaps should have – ridden safely to assure the result. But instead he went all-out, winning the final stage and taking the race victory in style. Walker has faced many terrible injuries and setbacks in his career but winners never give up.

STAGE STATS:

STAGES	DISTANCE (KM)	DESCENT (M)
5	**38**	**3000**

TIME CHECK:

FINAL RACE RESULTS

Men
1. Matthew Walker   35:24.95
2. Alex Rudeau   +16.59
3. Richie Rude   +18.33
4. Charles Murray   +19.68
5. Jesse Melamed   +22.42

Women
1. Isabeau Courdurier 41:03.36
2. Morgane Charre   +7.07
3. Mélanie Pugin   +17.37
4. Gloria Scarsi   +47.17
5. Hattie Harnden   +51

STAGE BY STAGE

STAGE 1
Men
1. Alex Rudeau   7:09.65
2. Richie Rude   +1.95
3. Rhys Verner   +4
Race Leader: Rudeau

Women
1. Isabeau Courdurier 8:09.68
2. Morgane Charre   +5.94
3. Mélanie Pugin   +7.94
Race Leader: Courdurier

STAGE 2
Men
1. Richie Rude   8:43.30
2. Jesse Melamed   +6.15
3. Matthew Walker   +8.45
Race Leader: Rude

Women
1. Hattie Harnden   10:21.28
2. Morgane Charre   +10
3. Chloe Taylor   +10.17
Race Leader: Courdurier

STAGE 3
Men
1. Alex Rudeau   4:58.73
2. Jesse Melamed   +0.98
3. Richie Rude   +4.97
Race Leader: Rude

Women
1. Isabeau Courdurier 5:45.96
2. Mélanie Pugin   +4.91
3. Gloria Scarsi   +4.92
Race Leader: Courdurier

STAGE 4
Men
1. Matthew Walker   10:49.42
2. Charles Murray   +4
3. Rhys Verner   +8.96
Race Leader: Walker

Women
1. Morgane Charre   12:25.75
2. Mélanie Pugin   +7.96
3. Isabeau Courdurier   +9
Race Leader: Charre

STAGE 5
Men
1. Matthew Walker   3:22.59
2. Charles Murray   +1.39
3. Richie Rude   +2.05

Women
1. Isabeau Courdurier 3:59.78
2. Mélanie Pugin   +4.92
3. Gloria Scarsi   +5.97

Through My Lens: The Evolution Of Enduro

Words: Anka Martin. Image: Sven Martin

Let me begin by admitting I'm old. I started racing 'enduro' before it was a thing – way before enduro-specific bikes, kit, tyres, and, yes, long before dropper posts. I wanted to get more out of riding my bike than just attending the Downhill World Cup races. So, I tried some multi-day marathon cross country events like Cape Epic, but it was a bit too much riding. I needed to find the middle ground. In our travels to Europe, like most downhillers at the time, we gave races like the Mega Avalanche and Mountain of Hell a crack. What an eye-opening experience. Fred Glo, French Enduro Series founder, and Enrico Guala, of the Italian Super Enduro Series, were pretty much responsible for creating a whole new racing discipline. I'd go so far as to say they changed my life.

Through these events, I met a great crew who tuned me into a new style of racing and riding developing in France and Italy. Jérôme and Pauline Clementz showed me the ropes. I tagged along with them to all the events, picking up invaluable tips and lessons. I was hooked, travelling to new destinations and immersing myself in new cultures. We rode for days and ate like kings and queens along the way, and as it turned out, I became pretty good at it, too. There was a lot to figure out: pacing

yourself, practising and preparing properly and choosing the right equipment for a week-long adventure.

Each year, the events grew bigger in numbers and participants. Bike development and component technology were progressing rapidly to keep up with the demands of these races. While the sport and bikes were rapidly evolving, we still looked like kooks at times, donning full-face helmets, sunglasses and backpacks. It was the privateer's dream: hanging out at massive van campsites, making friends, swapping stories and spares, and sharing line choices and crash stories. It was fun, social and amazing bang for your buck. By the end of the week, you knew you had ridden all the best tracks that a mountain or region had to offer. Sometimes the tracks didn't even exist before the race – proper trailblazing.

Fabien Barel's Urge Invitational in Cabo Verde Islands and Ash Smith's Trans-Provence (Now Stone King Rally) are standout events. They opened my eyes to proper rugged, multi-day adventuring, pushing the limits of what bike and body could accomplish. Meeting and riding alongside the sport's greatest – Tracy Moseley, Sabrina Jonnier, Nico Vouilloz, Hans

Rey, Mark Weir, Anne-Caroline Chausson, René Wildhaber, and Jérome, to name a few – was incredible.

Fast forward to 2013, a world series was launched: the Enduro World Series. We were lined up in Punta Ala, Italy, and nervous excitement ran high. There were many familiar faces, but new ones too, and the schedule was jam-packed with exotic locations – a true World Series. Over the next five years, we visited around 12 countries and 6 islands on 4 continents at about 23 venues (new and repeat) offering race stages aplenty. I finally found the racing discipline I had been looking for throughout my biking career. The 'Spirit of Enduro' was a thing, and the camaraderie at these races abounded. With multiple days of practice and racing, these events were physical, even when chairlifts were on offer. It seemed organisers aimed to one-up each other, vying for the title of the 'longest', 'hardest', 'most vertical' or 'technical' race ever.

As the world and industry caught on, racers became more serious and competitive. You could make a career of it. Sponsorships, salaries and professionalism levels skyrocketed, a natural progression in this

"The once-burning desire to explore and adventure seemed to have given way to spending hours indoors, studying GoPro footage or getting massages"

burgeoning enduro discipline. Along the way, the sport changed – pre-practice crept in, GoPros became the must-have accessory and walking the stages started.

The spirit of enduro had changed. The once-burning desire to explore and embark on adventures seemed to have given way to spending hours indoors, studying GoPro footage or getting massages. During one of my last EWS races, I remember waiting at the top of a stage, watching everyone check the upcoming track on their phones or GoPros. It was quiet, and the banter of the early days wasn't there. Times had changed, and along the way, the thing that had drawn me to enduro.

Results seemed to be more important than human connections. So, it was time for me to wrap up this chapter in my life.

The evolution of the discipline continued on an upward trajectory. Names and careers were built, salaries and team trucks grew, and more countries and venues were added to the calendar. It was fun to follow.

However, there have been recent significant changes as part of this evolution. I am happy that I raced during the EWS's adventure-fuelled ('glory') years, visiting international venues with trails that demanded big days out on the bike. Yet, I am somewhat saddened to see how

the sport's ethos and format have changed significantly: half-day races with a day for practice, often with repeat stages at repeat venues or venues not suited for backcountry enduro racing. Enduro stars are forced to play second fiddle to downhillers at some rounds, having to race midweek with no vibe or spectator presence. Hopefully, for the riders' sake, the series can find some of its original flame for the future.

I don't think that I am alone in having this sentiment. Luckily, there has been an explosion of the 'trans' style adventure races across the globe, where you can find the 'Spirit of Enduro' truly well and alive.

Screen Time

Words: Andy Lund. Image: Boris Beyer

I'm Andy Lund, head technician, road manager and man-on-the-ground for Trek Factory Racing (Enduro) Gravity and personal mechanic to Hattie Harnden.

The beat-your-number-board game was back on in 2023 after having finished third in the elite women's category overall in 2022 – we wanted to do even better in the first year of the UCI Mountain Bike Enduro World Cup.

Fast forward several months, and we have just finished the penultimate round of the 2023 season in Loudenvielle, France. Back into third in the overall – we wouldn't give up the number three plate without a fight.

We travelled 905km from Loudenvielle to Châtel for the final round of the series, a double event week alongside the Cross Country Marathon World Cup. The first Enduro World Cup within the Portes du Soleil area was highly anticipated. A popular holiday and riding destination, the venue contained it all. The stages ranged from finely sculpted, awkwardly taped bike park trails, creating a struggle to find flow, to the classic alpine meadow and fresh-scented forest singletrack.

Arriving in Châtel, we settled into a race week routine: setting up the bike on Tuesday, locating our pit space and prepping it for the week. Some of the views out of the office are better than others. Looking at thousand-metre-plus majestic mountains while working is something I do not take for granted. However, a distinct sense of autumn's imminent arrival in the Alps made for cool mornings and the requirement for a woolly hat.

An extra week from the previous race gave us time for further preparation, including a full bike strip down and rebuild. Double-checking through every component is a must before the first practice day. For racing, preparation is

vital and proper preparation prevents piss-poor performance – there are variations of this saying, but this is our favourite.

Suspension: a refresh from the ever-helpful guys at SRAM kept things running smoothly – fork pressure 70psi and shock 180psi.

Wheels: we went with a minimum of three sets. Identical setups, lacing, spoke tension, and tyres was our first practice option. The third set was a wet or intermediate option. We were racing in mid-September in the Alps, after all.

Tyre pressure: 21psi front and 23psi rear.

Brakes: we bled them and set the levers to a 55mm reach, adjusting the pad contact point for the full range and putting in sintered pads and new discs – brake bite: 33mm.

Transmission: we put on a new chain, charged AXS batteries and ran through all gears – shifting was good; no issues. Newly charged batteries went on the derailleur and seat post, with a spare battery in the tool roll – chainring size: 32tooth.

Practice was split into two days on the Thursday and Saturday before the race, a slightly different format to what we are used to, but the ability to adapt and overcome is a good thing. Practice went well. But overnight rain made Thursday's conditions slithery under tyre, spreading slick dirt onto rocks and creating low grip – braking points were key. With one run per stage, finding lines and building speed was crucial. Feedback from Hattie: 'Everything was all good.'

Coffee was first on the agenda from the busiest café in town on Saturday. A who's who of the enduro world spent time at Wood Cafe during the week. Good coffee and *pain au chocolat* got us going.

Up on the gondola and straight into the mix of the stages, we made no changes to the bike settings and pressures. Consistency and predictability were a high priority for Hattie, with such varied terrain and long days in the saddle – saddle height 73.3mm.

Often, I will ride practice to provide support on-stage, looking at and riding lines and having an identical bike for spare parts. Practice day was complete, with a minor hiccup creating extra work before Sunday's race. A thorough check was needed for the bike. I'd seated fresh tyres on race wheels since the start of the week and replaced discs (front and rear) for use with the sintered pads. I keep discs and race wheels separate for racing.

Arranging the pit set-up started early morning on race day. Working with Sam, our soigneur, food, water, and spare pieces of kit were on the tables – chocolate milk for the finish.

Final bolt check: done. Frame and wheel stickers: applied. Tyre pressure: set. Fork and shock settings: counted along with air pressure. Roll-out time: 10:23:30. Seven stages awaited and the final one started at 17:00:30 – over six hours of bike time were coming.

I spend most of a race day glued to my phone. My screen time goes through the roof, hitting refresh and watching the live timing. I can only provide support at an allocated time at the tech assistance zone if Hattie is not self-sufficient.

Hattie kept in touch throughout the day. Her stage times were good, maintaining that consistency, accruing stage points and riding smartly. Dropping into the last stage, she sat third on the day, a seven-second gap to fourth. Then, as she crossed the line, her time held. Happy days, with 2,333 points to secure a consecutive third in the season overall.

"Some of the views out of the office are better than others. Looking at thousand-metre-plus majestic mountains while working is something I do not take for granted"

01/09/

ROUND 6
LOUDENVIELLE
FRANCE

BORIS BEYER

Opposite: World enduro racing visited Loudenvielle for the third time in a row in 2023, but new this time was the addition of a downhill World Cup in the same week. The trails were as good as ever and fans enjoyed a week of festivities. Jesse Melamed kept it consistent, taking fifth in the race. Kevin Miquel finished 14th in the race.

ENDURO WORLD CUP / ROUND 6
LOUDENVIELLE-PEYRAGUDES / FRANCE / 01/09/2023
42.7957° N / 0.4127° E

01/09/2023
2023

SLOW AND STEADY WINS THE RACE

Round 6
Loudenvielle–Peyragudes
France
01/09/2023

SVEN MARTIN

Words: James Lumley-Parkin

Five rounds into the 2023 season, we'd already had five different winners on the men's side and a few new faces on the top of the box for the first time. With seasoned veterans battling it out with up-and-coming talent, the field was so strong it was hard for anyone to guess who would win this one. Well, apart from me, of course. I had called this win for the last four years at every round, and finally, I was on the money!

But we'll get to that later. Let me introduce Loudenvielle. The 'third time's a charm'; everyone seemed stoked to be back. Racing here has been fast and fierce, with stages providing plenty of variety to check all the enduro boxes. Rocks, check. Mud, check. Loam, check. Roots, well, that's a given. And the list goes on.

The sleepy town looks like a miniature dropped in the middle of a panorama of staggeringly high mountains and peaks. The 295 or so locals were again overrun by all things bikes, with the Pyrenees Bike Festival happening and the downhill World Cup circus sharing this little, not-so-hidden-any-more gem with the enduro squad.

After a two-month break since Val di Fassa, riders were eager to get back between the tape. Had they used this time off wisely, training hard, or were they caught up in chill summer vibes? There was only one way to find out.

Not much had changed since 2022: the stages remained the same, with minor tweaks and additions. That said, if it ain't broke! In 'only' five stages, this place packs so much variety, from fast, open alpine singletrack and smooth bike park turns to terrifyingly steep rootfests deep in the native forests.

Home soil advantage is never brought up more than here in France. Last year, the nine French in the top 20 men's field and the clean French sweep of the women's podium testified. Would it be the same again this year? Or would the familiarity even the playing field?

Practice was on Thursday, with the race scheduled for Saturday. Mist and clouds hung heavily in the

early morning air down in town. Fortunately, the first gondola broke through the inverted cloud cover and the impressive mountain ranges above were bathed in sunlight. The morning's moisture had coated the tracks. It was going to be a bit slick out there. Although the stages slowly dried throughout the day, pockets of moisture kept riders on their toes.

Before racing began, the highlight for many was seeing Iago Garay, one of enduro's OGs, back on a bike after the shocking brain aneurysm he suffered at the Pietra Ligure round. It was good to see him ripping again – not racing – being the steeziest team manager on the circuit.

With the stages drying out over practice, the promise of a race to remember looked good. A forecast electrical storm on Saturday almost put a spanner in the works before the tough decision to move the race to Friday. With no rest after practice, we got stuck straight in.

Some may have been a bit disgruntled to miss a day to recover (special shoutout to team mechanics who must have burned some midnight oil to get race rigs ready), but boy, were we lucky with the weather. Friday rolled in with the sun blazing across a clear blue sky.

Having practiced the day before, riders entered the first stage with a good idea of what to expect. Most races this year had seen the amateurs race the day before the World Cup, often churning up the tracks to an almost unrecognisable level.

"WITH SEASONED VETERANS BATTLING IT THE FIELD WAS SO STRONG IT WAS HARD WIN THIS ONE"

SVEN MARTIN

Stage two, Nabias, was on the same side of the valley but required riders to ride back up and beyond the Col d'Azet. The stage started on a flatter, open hillside with incredible views overlooking Loudenvielle and the lake below. Riders wouldn't have much time to enjoy the panorama as they abruptly dropped into steeper stuff when they hit the tree line. Once again, thick tree coverage meant the track was still a little slick in places and would catch you out if you merely blinked at the wrong time. With the stage finishing closer to the valley floor, the crowds gathered. You don't have to speak the language to feel the encouragement from classic phrases such as hop hop hop and allez, pédale!

The riders jumped into a shuttle to haul them up to Col d'Azet, a good portion of the first climb. They still had a steep fire road pedal to stage one, Courtalets. Making more use of the vert available, the stage started higher than in previous years, stretching it to 2.8km with nearly 500m of vertical. Straight out the gate was a narrow alpine walking trail traversing the luscious green hillside – keep those pedals level! Racers had other things to worry about. Local cows caused havoc on the track, forcing riders to take exciting lines to avoid running into them. About one-third of the way down, and after a few short, punchy climbs, we dropped into the meat of the stage – lots of roots and slick mud. As predicted, the French started in force. Isabeau Courdurier added another stage win to her CV, whereas Louis Jeandel scored his very first. Richie Rude was 4.5 seconds back, closely followed by Youn Deniaud, hungry for a result he knew was within his reach. Last year's winner, Alex Rudeau, slipped out on an unassuming greasy corner, costing him precious seconds.

Riders crossed over to the Peyragudes side of the valley, hopping on the gondola up to the newly built downhill track, then up a chairlift to the highest point of the day for stage three. Val d'Aube was the longest stage of the day, just shy of 6km with 820m of elevation loss, with bike park berms up top but with a healthy dose of loose rock that caused several punctures. Near the end of the stage were some new, fresh grass turns. It wouldn't be a proper French race without them.

Only two seconds separated the now race favourites Rudeau and Deniaud on this five-and-a-half-minute stage. However, bursting the French bubble, a back-on-form Jack Moir took the stage win. Courdurier dominated with three out of three stage wins, but hot on her heels was fellow compatriot Morgane Charre, the 2022 winner. Ella Conolly was battling back at the top after a tough few months. However, her timing chips weren't relaying her times, so no-one would know how well she was doing until the end of the race.

OUT WITH UP-AND-COMING TALENT, FOR ANYONE TO GUESS WHO WOULD

Stage three rolled almost straight into stage four, Porticou, the shortest but steepest stage of the day. Weaving through dense forest, the light was scarce, making it hard to make out the web of roots running down the steep, sketchy sections. Riders reached warp speed as manicured berms caught them at the bottom of chutes and slingshotted them into the next section. This shorter stage seemed to favour some of the most experienced racers, with Jesse Melamed taking the stage win, closely followed by Martin Maes, happy to be back at the pointy end.

With only one stage to go, you may wonder, 'What's the deal with the title of this piece?'. It's a bit of an exaggeration, I admit, seeing as the racing was incredibly fast and loose. But this is where Deniaud steps in. He hadn't won a stage yet and felt, in his words, as if he was going slow. He decided not to look at the times before the big climb to the last stage – a wise decision as there were only mere tenths in it. I was nervous; I have had the pleasure of filming for the Giant Factory Off-Road Team for the past five years and followed Youn for four of those. (Editor note: does this constitute an ad?) I always knew he had it in him; he needed to hold it together for one more stage. Crashes, mechanicals and maybe a lack of luck have kept him off the podium, even though he is a top-ten contender at almost all races.

Stage five, Kern, was a gnarly mishmash of all we had seen. There was so much at stake on this relatively short 2.4km stage. Courdurier finished what she had started, winning four of the stages and taking her fourth victory of the year. Charre and Conolly had been battling for second all day, unbeknownst to the latter. We finally discovered Conolly's stage times only after the race had finished, landing her in an amazing third.

The tension grew as the men's field thinned, and the home crowd buzzed at the prospect of another French win. Even though Rudeau took the last stage, he couldn't match the speed and consistency of Deniaud. He had finally held it together, playing it smart and not pushing too hard, landing on his first World Cup podium and taking the win. Jeandel had backed up his early morning stage win with a standout performance throughout the day and slotted into third, just behind Rudeau.

So, make that six rounds and six different winners. Going into the season's last round, it would be anyone's guess who would win it. As for me, I'm done with predictions. I can rest easy now. Well done, Youn.

Alex Rudeau won here in 2022, his first Enduro World Series win. While he couldn't quite match that result in 2023, he was delighted with another standout ride in front of a home crowd. Second place for Rudeau, less than one second off the win after more than 26 minutes of racing.

SVEN MARTIN

BORIS BEYER

Here: How are ground conditions looking? Despite this near-death moment, Greg Callaghan raced to 37th place. **Opposite:** A consistent day put Harriet Harnden fourth in the race and moved her into third in the season standings going into the last round. **Below:** What a beautiful view. No, not the scenery. The highlight of Loudenvielle was seeing Iago Garay back riding and styling things up during practice after suffering a brain aneurysm while racing at round three.

CELIN MARTIN

BORIS BEYER

BORIS BEYER

"THE SLEEPY TOWN LOOKS LIKE A MINIATURE DROPPED IN A PANORAMA OF STAGGERINGLY HIGH MOUNTAINS"

BORIS BEYER

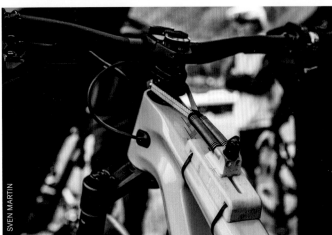

SVEN MARTIN

SVEN MARTIN

Opposite: Commencal's Louis Jeandel had the ride of his life and a best-ever result here, winning a stage and finishing third on an all-French podium.
Other photos: Enduro tech. Commencal brought out the telemetry systems at the 2023 World Cups, probably making them the first team to use data logging to help set up team bikes during an enduro race weekend.

SVEN MARTIN

SEBASTIAN SCHIECK

BORIS BEYER

Here and above: This one hurt. Jack Moir was leading the race going into the fifth and final stage, but some missing course marking tape made him go off-course and then climb back up the hill to rejoin the track where he left it (tyre marks visible on his GoPro video made it clear that other racers hadn't been so honest). Moir finished the day in sixth, gutted. **Opposite top:** Loudenvielle's enduro race was brought forward a day to the Friday of the World Cup bonanza weekend due to forecast storms on the Saturday. Luckily, racers enjoyed favourable conditions all week. Lisandru Bertini put in another solid ride to win the Under-21 category. **Opposite bottom:** Morgane Charre won here in 2022 and showed her speed again in 2023, this time settling for second place and another decent haul of series points.

SVEN MARTIN

BORIS BEYER

Isabeau Courdurier did her thing to take the race win and hold onto the series lead, but Morgane Charre had been pushing her hard all year and the two Frenchies at the top would take the title chase all the way to the final race.

BORIS BEYER

SVEN MARTIN

SVEN MARTIN

SVEN MARTIN

"WITH ONLY ONE STAGE TO GO, YOU MAY WONDER, 'WHAT'S THE DEAL WITH THE TITLE OF THIS PIECE?"

SVEN MARTIN

Unreal. Youn Deniaud had shown promise for years and our reporter had money on him for a race win. But no matter how skilled and prepared a racer is, there's little that can prepare them for the reality of a first-ever World Cup win. Deniaud kept it consistent all day to move up through the ranks until there was no higher place to go. And the crowd went wild.

BORIS BEYER

BORIS BEYER

STAGE STATS:

STAGES	DISTANCE (KM)	DESCENT (M)
5	37.5	3170

TIME CHECK:

FINAL RACE RESULTS

Men

1. Youn Deniaud   26:17.67
2. Alex Rudeau   +0.74
3. Louis Jeandel   +1.63
4. Richie Rude   +8.48
5. Jesse Melamed   +8.61

Women

1. Isabeau Courdurier   29:40.88
2. Morgane Charre   +22.66
3. Ella Conolly   +32.47
4. Hattie Harnden   +1:33.45
5. Noga Korem   +1:35.62

STAGE BY STAGE

STAGE 1

Men

1. Louis Jeandel   5:54.88
2. Richie Rude   +4.96
3. Youn Deniaud   +7.92
Race Leader: Jeandel

Women

1. Isabeau Courdurier   6:52.6
2. Ella Conolly   +4.21
3. Mélanie Pugin   +6.44
Race Leader: Courdurier

STAGE 2

Men

1. Alex Rudeau   6:23.75
2. Youn Deniaud   +2.97
3. Louis Jeandel   +5.96
Race Leader: Jeandel

Women

1. Isabeau Courdurier   7:12.70
2. Ella Conolly   +8.01
3. Morgane Charre   +9.8
Race Leader: Courdurier

STAGE 3

Men

1. Jack Moir   5:32.27
2. Alex Rudeau   +2.41
3. Youn Deniaud   +4.32
Race Leader: Rudeau

Women

1. Isabeau Courdurier   6:12.70
2. Ella Conolly   +5.98
3. Morgane Charre   +7
Race Leader: Courdurier

STAGE 4

Men

1. Jesse Melamed   2:46.08
2. Martin Maes   +0.51
3. Jack Moir   +0.52
Race Leader: Moir

Women

1. Isabeau Courdurier   3:10.32
2. Morgane Charre   +3.98
3. Ella Conolly   +4.97
Race Leader: Courdurier

STAGE 5

Men

1. Alex Rudeau   5:20.76
2. Jesse Melamed   +1.97
3. Louis Jeandel   +2.13

Women

1. Morgane Charre   6:08.39
2. Isabeau Courdurier   +4.17
3. Ella Conolly   +14.32

On The Edge

Words: Romain Paulhan. Images: Sven Martin

Despite my mind being consumed with thoughts about the downhill track on a nearby slope, I was on my Bronson bike, practicing for the Enduro (EDR) World Cup in Loudenvielle. The stages were beautiful, and the conditions ideal – good weather, technical terrain and perfect dirt. I turned my focus to the race. My worries dissipated as I navigated the stages and felt in tune with my bike. Notwithstanding the distractions, I finished 13th – my best EDR World Cup result.

I could assume that it was because I rode the trails during the month I spent working there, but I guess not, since the two trails we rode in the evening with Jasmine and Baptiste, both of whom were very involved in the Pyrenees Bike Festival, are the ones where I got the worst results. Go figure.

As I finished my race, satisfied, my mind returned to work. I received a text from Amaury Pierron: 'Bravo Paulhette, too good! We need to do something about the landing on the last gap. Thomas broke a crank arm and someone else a pedal.'

Having the chance to create an entire World Cup downhill track and to see the world's best compete on it has been a dream come true.

It all started last year when Ludovic Henry, the project manager for the Loudenvielle Downhill World Cup, called me and said, 'Romain, I need you to build this track. I want quality work. I know you have experience. Pompon and Bruni

told me I can count on you. Would you be up for it?'

A month later, at the end of autumn, we were walking the track. The layout had been pre-defined. All that was left to do was to fine-tune the sections we thought were the most interesting and put some flow into it all.

The stakes were high. The track had to be built across 1.6km of challenging terrain. The canvas wasn't ideal for creativity, with a grassy and open upper section subject to wind and fog and a steep main section with a single slope and off-camber. However, after walking the slope several times, the ideas matured.

To avoid spending five months on site, I requested to work with Mountain Lines, a local company that helped create the area's bike park trails. I supervised their manual shaping while I worked on the sections requiring an excavator.

ESO Sport's (the World Cup series organiser) specifications were simple: they wanted a fast, steep, challenging track with a clear b-zone. Personally, I prefer technical tracks that flow, where speeds remain reasonable and riding on the edge while pushing the limits is enjoyable.

And so, it began. My first shovelful at the start of April 2023 was filled with nervous excitement. I faced a huge challenge, and I told myself, 'Come on, now we've got to get it right... the whole world is looking on.'

The most challenging part of this project was overseeing the work of the build team. This entailed effectively conveying my precise vision for the trail, specifying the positioning and dimensions of the catch-berms on the off-camber sections, and planning the excavation of flat areas, using a pickaxe to make the tricky sections doable in case of rain.

After over five months of work and some 200 hours in the digger, we were set for the test event in mid-July to assess any necessary changes before the World Cup race that was set for early September. This test was crucial to ensure we didn't face any unexpected challenges on the big day.

I had given my final instructions to the build team in mid-May, and I arrived a few days before the test event and thought, 'This is borderline, we're not ready!'

Stumps and branches were scattered across the b-zone, but we needed to set a good example as a new venue, especially in France, and out of respect for my friend Amaury, who had been injured by debris at the first round of racing in Lenzerheide. So for two days, I gave it my all to try to make the test as safe as possible.

Opinions were mixed but positive overall during the first test rides: good flow on the top section but difficult to ride the lower parts.

During the debrief, Ludovic and I insisted that the b-zone and the lower section needed to be

finished and that we needed to have everything really dialled, especially after Amaury's accident earlier in the season. The riders were clear about it: I can recall telling Thomas Estaque, who was determined to make this round in the Pyrenees a celebration, saying, 'All the work remains to be done. The lower part looks like a teenager's track. It's not pro here.'

That's when the countdown began. I wrote an email clearly explaining the work that needed to be done. Ludovic and I even considered rebuilding another team because there was so much to do. He then asked Mountain Lines to remove the catch-berms, initially built with clumps of dirt and dead wood, and to rebuild them with stones and fresh dirt and wood. The message was clear and it worked out.

I returned a few days later to rework the final section because, as it was, it wasn't particularly spectacular. I spent three days on the digger, and the young bike park team lent me a hand with the clearing.

Fast forward to early September, and everything seemed ready. Ludovic asked me to verify the track for the umpteenth time. Everything looked good, though still not great, especially the b-zone. To my surprise, the ESO team didn't even come to check if the track was okay before the Andorra round. In any case, the die had been cast.

After racing the EDR World Cup race, I called Jean Phillipe Pellieu, manager of SLTS company located a few kilometres away. He called up his team and provided us with equipment so that I could finish work without asking for anything in return. In his words, it was 'for the beauty of the sport.'

There I was again, with the excavator's joysticks in my hands until 9pm working on the landing of the last gap. A very rainy night ensued, and the junior training sessions were put on hold the next day. We spent eight hours shovelling and digging with a team of volunteers

assembled on the spot to rework the berms and fill in the holes that had formed over the last few days.

The elite race went off without a glitch in glorious sunshine, and the many thank you messages and positive comments I received will forever remain the greatest reward of this challenge.

Heartfelt thanks to Ludo for his incredible involvement in this project; Jean Phillipe for his invaluable help; Jasmine and Baptiste for all the good times; Kila for her passion, her work and the incredible ride in the Aure Valley; and David for his involvement and outstanding work.

Special thanks also go to Stéphane for his understanding and to all the people who lent a hand in making this first edition a party, particularly Pablo and Flo for their help on the pickaxe, David for the coordination, and, of course, all the volunteers.

"I prefer technical tracks that flow,
where the speed remains reasonable,
and riding on the edge while pushing
the limits of speed is enjoyable"

ROUND 7 CHATEL FRANCE

Opposite: Thomas Lapeyrie raced in every year of the Enduro World Series–Enduro World Cups bar one (2022), but in Châtel he announced his retirement from world-level racing after a long career on the circuit.

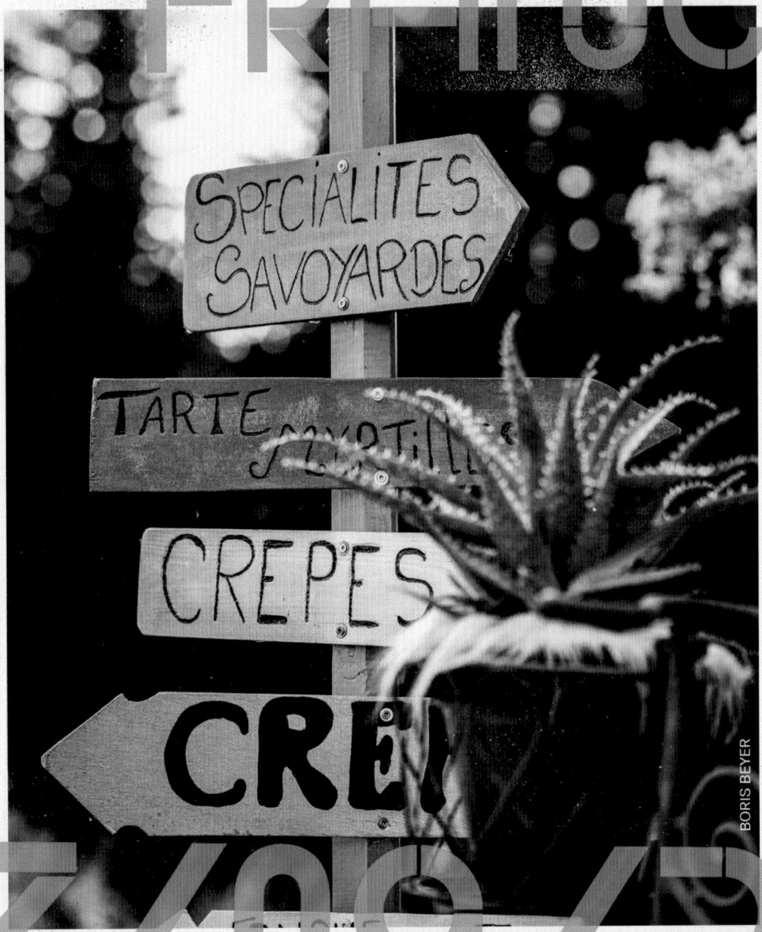

SPECIALITES SAVOYARDES

TARTE MYRTILLES

CREPES

CRE

BORIS BEYER

17/09/202
/09/2023

ANY WHICH WAY

Round 7
Châtel
France
17/09/2023

SVEN MARTIN

Words: James McKnight

SVEN MARTIN

One day on a bicycle. A simple run around some mountains. Just seven trails, and your season's done. Does that sound easy? Probably not, but even making a point about the difficulty of racing an Enduro World Cup isn't easy (here's another try: the final round would have almost as much racing time as an entire season of downhill World Cup race runs added together).

SVEN MARTIN

Anyway, the EDRers showed up at the final round in Châtel, France, with little idea what lay ahead. Perhaps a set of bike park tracks, the ultimate nightmare of every racer worrying that the death of a sport is a single whacker-plated trail away? Châtel, the venue, is a bike park, after all. But rumours had it that the course shapers had been cooking up a storm, with tracks dotted all over the place on different slopes, each with unique features and dirt.

The trail builders had indeed conjured up perhaps the best set of stages of the season with the help of a mystery local known only as the Trail Farmer. From nasty greasy root fests near the village of Châtel to flat-out downhill tracks near Morzine, to grimy boulder-strewn numbers near Avoriaz and back to Pré la Joux (Châtel's bike park area about ten mins from the town) all via challenging and progressive hand-shaped tracks. The season was ending on a high.

Coming into the event, the series titles were still wide open in men's and women's elite categories. Isabeau Courdurier, going for a third series title, had a convincing lead, but if she had a bad race and Morgane Charre went well, the title could still go to Charre. In the men's, Richie Rude was also going for a third series win (amazingly, despite having the most male EWS wins in history by far, his last title had been in 2016). But Rude's points lead coming into Châtel was by no means enough for him to cruise this one home – Alex Rudeau, Jesse Melamed and Rhys Verner weren't far behind, and the title could still go in any direction.

Whoever sealed the deal on the series here would end the year crowned as the first UCI Enduro World Cup overall winner (reminder for anyone living under a rock: the Enduro World Series ran for ten seasons from 2013-2022 before enduro became an official UCI discipline and changed its name to the Enduro World Cup in 2023). Aside from the kudos, there was also a big new football World Cup-esque trophy waiting for whoever finished on top. Riders ready? Let's go.

Finishing the season consistently inconsistently, the race schedule was set for two days of practice spread out with a rest day in between (on this day, the amateur enduro took to the course, racing all but one of the EDR stages), then racing the following day. This gave racers ample time to get accustomed to their surroundings and hang out at Wood Café or Nazca Bar – basically the only two places open at this late point in the resort's season. Float around town for a coffee or burger, and you'd likely bump into the stars of enduro and a handful of top-tier downhillers who were either there to support their friends and team-mates or try their hand at enduro. With barely any fans around during the week, it felt like a grassroots gathering of mountain biking's elite, some of them with their guard down, some with their eyes on a prize.

Despite the race's use of six different chairlifts and gondolas during the day, Châtel was no easy ride – racers would cover about 60km distance with 800m

"RUMOURS HAD IT THAT THE SHAPERS WITH TRACKS DOTTED ALL OVER THE PLACE ON DIFFERENT SLOPES"

of climbing and a chunky 3,600m of descending. At race pace, those numbers equate to a lot of panting, sweating and probably the odd bit of cursing.

Setting out early morning from the foot of the bike park's deep, steep valley, racers made their way to the first stage via a lift and some pedalling. This track was a hand-cut feast of loamy, rooty brilliance that some called the year's best stage. Standing trackside, seeing the sport's elite ripping around turns and cutting across cambers – well, it was the sort of stuff that makes you want to go and ride a bike. Courdurier and Melamed got the day off to a flying start with the stage wins here. Melamed was making a statement and chasing the series title; Courdurier was protecting her series lead. Both were charging hard.

Stage two was quite a different affair – just as full of dusty, techy treats, but with a sting in its tail in the form of a brutal sprint. Starting in the high Alpine somewhere above the town of Châtel, the trail went full speed through meadows with long, fast turns before diving into the woods and some tighter, flat corners. Melamed went well again, earning a second stage win, and Harriet Harnden stepped into the ring in the women's, taking the stage and building momentum towards a solid overall result.

Into the thick of it. Col du Saix, stage three, was the hardest of the day, with a barrage of off-cambers, thick spider webs of tree roots, abundant trees, and rocks waiting to catch a shoulder or pedal. As former downhill World Cup winner Josh Bryceland noted in practice (he was racing the E-EDR), getting down unscathed would take a heroic ride. Courdurier slipped up and came to a brief stop on-course, but she battled on to take the stage win. Now it was time for Rudeau to shine, his flat pedal riding and unrivalled technical skills carrying him to the stage win. Courdurier and Charre were head-to-head in the fight for the race win; Rude, on the other hand, wasn't feeling the flow, and his series title looked up for grabs.

From three to four was a long-haul journey over the mountains via a pit-stop at the, er, pits, several chairlifts, one massive descent and a traverse to somewhere above Morzine. This stage was a timeless classic of the area, Hattock. This track has been chopped and changed over the years, but its spirit remains the same – fast through the trees, perfectly shaped berms, slightly greasy top-layer, some jumps and plenty of roots. Perfect terrain for an ex-downhill racer; indeed, Charre and Jack Moir – with many seasons of downhill World Cup experience – stepped up to take the stage wins.

Stage five dropped down from Avoriaz into Les Lindarets on the old French Cup downhill track – which used to be the height of sketchy technicality, but these days is a fast blast mid-enduro race. Charre again set the pace... but no! Well, yes. Hang on, what? Charre and Courdurier scored precisely the same time on this stage – down to the thousandths. Had that ever happened before? Who knows, but it'd soon happen again (stay tuned). The French duo kept their positions at the front of the pack in the race overall in one of the tightest battles of the season. Melamed went well through the rocks and rough stuff and scored another stage win, but this time, Rude was just behind him and showing signs of resurgence, pushing hard, foot out in turns and positive at the end of his run.

HAD BEEN COOKING UP A STORM,

One of Châtel bike park's most esteemed trails, Haute Tension, brought riders back within a stone's throw of the finish for the penultimate stage. Snaking across and then plunging down the top of the valley, the track is a mix of shaped and raw terrain, with high lines through shrubbery sending riders at full pace into perfectly sculpted chest-high berms that link one to the next seamlessly. Charre and Courdurier again came out on top, this time to Courdurier's advantage but only by a slim margin. Another flat pedal rider, Dan Booker, stepped into the mix, taking the men's win and compressing the top-five overall times. Shout out to downhill pro Dylan Levesque, battling with the enduro specialists in the top ten.

Charre went into the final stage with a slight two-second lead over Courdurier in the overall after 25 minutes of racing. Some 20 seconds back, Harnden sat in third, but Ella Conolly was just six seconds behind her. Melamed held a lead of eight seconds over Rudeau, but Rude and Booker were sitting third and fourth with only two hundredths of a second separating them. Rude and Courdurier's titles looked good, but they'd still need a solid ride on stage seven, the last of the year.

After a quick transfer and break between stages, racers dived into the stage that would bring them back into the start-finish area, where fans, team and media gathered to welcome them home. But not before a final blast on a short track full of hard hits and dust-filled turns – enough for a last-minute crash or breakage.

Charre's confidence had been building all day, and she peaked with a final stage win on seven, giving her the race win. Courdurier left nothing on the hill

and rallied to second on the stage, second in the race and first in the series, an incredible third title hers for the keeping after a long and demanding season. Harnden ended her day third in the race and third in the series – another achievement on the young racer's impressive multi-discipline resume.

Like Charre in the women's, Melamed kept it lit to take the stage win and wrap up the race in style, ending his season with a victory and second place in the series standings. Rude took no chances on the last track with a safe ride to secure his third EWS-EDR title. Rudeau took second in the race and was ecstatic to step onto the podium for the fifth time in the season, his consistency putting him third in the series overall.

Slawomir Lukasik and Booker rounded out the top five in the men's race with the exact same overall times – after 24 minutes of competition, there wasn't even a thousandth of a second's difference in their riding. If anyone thought enduro was anything but edge-of-seat exciting, they needed to think again: the year's racing had been arguably tighter, faster and more varied than ever. For us fans, it had been a total pleasure to watch. Thank you to all the riders risking life and limb putting on such a fantastic show. Long may it continue!

Jesse Melamed came into the 2023 season as the reigning champion but moving to a new team (Canyon) after literally decades with his previous sponsor (Rocky Mountain) was never going to be easy. Melamed and his team worked relentlessly through the off-season and came in hot, racking up decent results all season and ending the year in on a high in Châtel with the race win and second in the series overall.

SEBASTIAN SCHIECK

SVEN MARTIN

Here: Rooty, loamy, dusty, gritty, grimy, slippery, hardpacked, loose, muddy, easy, hard, treacherous – Châtel's course had something for every taste. But get it wrong and it could bite hard, as Andréane Lanthier-Nadeau found out. **Opposite top:** Mélanie Pugin had a mostly consistent season comfortably inside the top-ten at all but two races. She finished fifth here and sixth in the series overall. **Opposite bottom:** The tech challenges came hard and fast on Châtel's seven stages. Noga Korem held it together for seventh in the race. **Below:** When the going gets tech, the flat pedals get going. Dan Booker kept it feet-up to take fifth in the race – but there's a caveat. See Sławomir Łukasik's caption later in this report.

SVEN MARTIN

SVEN MARTIN

SVEN MARTIN

"SEEING THE SPORT'S ELITE RIPPING TURNS AND CAMBERS MAKES YOU WANT TO RIDE A BIKE"

SVEN MARTIN

BORIS BEYER

Opposite and above: Teamwork makes it all possible. Harriet Harnden's season finished on a strong note here, with third in the race and third in the series overall. Her mechanic, Andy Lund, is another key figure on the enduro scene (his feature elsewhere in this book gives some insight into the process behind a podium result).
Below: Simona Kuchyňková rounded off the year with the win in Under-21. The Slovakian missed three races in the series but still managed sixth in the overall rankings.

BORIS BEYER

SVEN MARTIN

SEBASTIAN SCHIECK

Opposite: Sławomir Łukasik and Dan Booker had exactly the same overall time here – down to the thousandths. Łukasik's stage points gave him an advantage over Booker though and he finished one place ahead in the results. **Above and below:** Isabeau Courdurier battled with Morgane Charre all day, the duo so close that they even had the exact same time on stage five (again, down to the thousandths). Courdurier had a sizeable lead in the series points, but she needed to stay on her toes to ensure the victory. She did that, finishing second in the race to take her third championship. Courdurier's been racing at this level since the first Enduro World Series in 2013 and Châtel was her 50th career podium – respect.

SVEN MARTIN

BORIS BEYER

Opposite and below: Three second places and five podiums in a row put Alex Rudeau firmly in third in the final series rankings. Not bad when you consider he only started racing in 2019. Rudeau's background in bicycle trials (he rode at world-level in that discipline too) has earnt him supreme technical skills that, when coupled with the lightning speed he's built year-on-year, make him one of the riders to beat at any and every venue.

SVEN MARTIN

"THE YEAR'S RACING HAD BEEN ARGUABLY TIGHTER, FASTER AND MORE VARIED THAN EVER"

SVEN MARTIN

Here and opposite: Despite being the winningest male in enduro history by far with 19 Enduro World Series-Enduro World Cup wins (Jesse Melamed is the closest to Rude in total wins with eight wins including Châtel), Rude hadn't scored a series title since 2016. Leading the series rankings coming into Châtel, he needed a solid ride to ensure the title; the attacks came from every angle and the day started slowly by his standards – he said he was struggling to get in the flow. But champions simply have that extra something that elevates them to another level when the pressure's on. Rude regrouped and gave it hell on the last stages, wrapping up the day in third and taking his third series title. **Below:** Ella Conolly faced injury and worse in 2023, but she kept it positive and was always in the mix. She finished the season with a fourth in Châtel and seventh in the series despite missing two rounds.

SVEN MARTIN

SVEN MARTIN

SVEN MARTIN

BORIS BEYER

Opposite and top: Morgane Charre pushed Isabeau Courdurier right to the very end, the two locked in battle throughout Châtel's race in one of the tightest series finals we can remember. Charre was elated to take the win on the day and second in the overall rankings. **Above:** Both these riders rode in the very first Enduro World Series in 2013. Fabien Barel (right) won the opening race that year; in 2023, his expertise as Canyon's team manager helped Jesse Melamed (left) give it full gas at the last round in Châtel, winning four of the seven stages and the race overall. The result put Melamed second in the final series rankings. What a way to end the year.

SVEN MARTIN

STAGE STATS:

STAGES	DISTANCE (KM)	DESCENT (M)
7	**58**	**3600**

TIME CHECK:

FINAL RACE RESULTS

Men
1. Jesse Melamed — 23:57.73
2. Alex Rudeau — +11.48
3. Richie Rude — +24.78
4. Sławomir Łukasik — +24.86
5. Dan Booker — +24.86

Women
1. Morgane Charre — 27:54.41
2. Isabeau Courdurier — +6.87
3. Hattie Harnden — +33.35
4. Ella Conolly — +36.01
5. Mélanie Pugin — +48.33

STAGE BY STAGE

STAGE 1
Men
1. Jesse Melamed — 2:59.78
2. Dan Booker — +3.01
3. Jack Menzies — +3.94
Race Leader: Melamed

Women
1. Isabeau Courdurier — 3:32.97
2. Morgane Charre — +0.99
3. Barbora Vojta — +5.91
Race Leader: Courdurier

STAGE 2
Men
1. Jesse Melamed — 4:37.03
2. Alex Rudeau — +0.11
3. Sławomir Łukasik — +0.44
Race Leader: Melamed

Women
1. Hattie Harnden — 5:28.35
2. Gloria Scarsi — +0.99
3. Morgane Charre — +2.99
Race Leader: Charre

STAGE 3
Men
1. Alex Rudeau — 3:50.90
2. Charles Murray — +1.92
3. Jesse Melamed — +3.96
Race Leader: Melamed

Women
1. Isabeau Courdurier — 4:36.60
2. Morgane Charre — +0.98
3. Hattie Harnden — +2.98
Race Leader: Courdurier

STAGE 4
Men
1. Jack Moir — 3:07.52
2. Jesse Melamed — +0.95
3. Richie Rude — +1.08
Race Leader: Melamed

Women
1. Morgane Charre — 3:31.19
2. Isabeau Courdurier — +2.98
3. Ella Conolly — +4.44
Race Leader: Charre

STAGE 5
Men
1. Jesse Melamed — 3:42.31
2. Richie Rude — +2.66
3. Kasper Woolley — +4.39
Race Leader: Melamed

Women
1. Morgane Charre — 4:16.73
2. Isabeau Courdurier — +0
3. Ella Conolly — +3.96
Race Leader: Charre

STAGE 6
Men
1. Dan Booker — 3:05.65
2. Alex Rudeau — +1.95
3. Jack Moir — +1.98
Race Leader: Melamed

Women
1. Isabeau Courdurier — 3:32.85
2. Morgane Charre — +0.92
3. Ella Conolly — +2.97
Race Leader: Charre

STAGE 7
Men
1. Jesse Melamed — 2:28.46
2. Sławomir Łukasik — +1.33
3. Jack Moir — +2.02

Women
1. Morgane Charre — 2:50.91
2. Isabeau Courdurier — +4.98
3. Ella Conolly — +7.93

Zoe Cuthbert: 22, A Van, And Some World Cups

Words: Léo Kervran. Images: Paul Humbert

Cross country (XC) World Cups are expensive and far away, especially when you don't have a team and come from the other side of the planet. But for Zoe Cuthbert, that's no reason to give up.

At just 22, the Australian is the only rider on the XC circuit living in a van to spend the season in Europe and race at the highest level. She also turns her hand to other disciplines, including enduro World Cups, 4X and a stint at Crankworx.

The following interview by our friends at Vojo Magazine (our favourite French cycling media – go check them out) is a glimpse into Zoe's world, the world of privateers in XC. The interview took place at the Les Gets round of the 2023 XC World Cup.

Vojo Magazine: Hello Zoe. To start with, can you tell us about yourself and how you first got into cycling?
Zoe Cuthbert: I'm an Australian rider from Canberra, the unknown capital. When I was six, my mum took me to a children's race; she was doing the 'grown up race', and there was one for the kids at the same time. I dropped my chain and came last, but I immediately asked her to sign me up for the next one so I could race again and pretty much fell in love with it.

I've always been very competition-focused; I started following my own training programmes at ten and always wanted to aim higher and

compete in bigger races. For a long time, my main goal was the National Championships; I did all the national rounds. Then I went abroad, to the World Championships and now on the World Cup circuit. I've always been looking for the next step, and I love it.

Vojo: Speaking of competition, you mainly race in XC, but you also took part in several Enduro World Cups this season, and you raced in 4X last year in Val di Sole... Do you easily switch between disciplines?
ZC: Yeah, I really love cycling. I've done track and road, played bike polo for a bit, and due to a bunch of random circumstances, I'm also the Australian national pump track champion; I did downhill at the national championships this year. I love cycling and competing, and I have loads of friends who do different disciplines, so they introduce me to new things. Last year, I came to Europe with my XC bike and couldn't spend six months without doing enduro, so I also brought my enduro and competed in the last two EWS races. I loved it, so I decided to do them again this year, the ones I could fit into the XC calendar. In the end, I think I did all the EWS except for two.

Vojo: And it seems to be working out! The last time you did an Enduro World Cup and an XC World Cup the week after, it went well, your first top-five of the year (in Lenzerheide, after the EDR in Finale Ligure).
ZC: I hope that's the secret! I did one last week, so hopefully, it'll be the same this

weekend. I really like Les Gets. I know it's not the most popular course, but I don't know, I feel good there.

Vojo: In recent years, everyone says that XC is becoming increasingly technical, and we see riders who succeed in being efficient in XC and enduro, like Hattie Harden. Generally speaking, there are more often crossovers between disciplines. Do you think this is something people should do more regularly?
ZC: Yes, I really do. Others might have a different opinion, but in my view, it's a great thing to mix it all up. Many people train on the road, which works too, or in CX... I think doing another discipline allows you to train while staying motivated and developing skills you might not have focused on otherwise. I believe enduro has greatly helped me in my power and technique. It's just a good way to have a big bike day in a style different from XC.

Vojo: You mentioned that you were already in Europe last year. Was it your first time? The World Cup is mainly centred on Europe, so coming from Australia, it's a significant journey. You go and live half the year in Europe.
ZC: Yes, but it's nice because we have the eternal summer! We return home, and it's summer, come back, and it's summer again. But this means most people from the southern hemisphere spend half their life travelling as long as they are competing. It can be cool and

"I believe enduro has greatly helped me in my power and technique. It's just a good way to have a big bike day in a style different from XC"

fun but also super hectic, and it's hard to be constantly on the move for so long.

Vojo: Why the choice of living in a van? From the outside, it doesn't seem the easiest for racing in World Cups.

ZC: I have many friends who did it for enduro last year, and it seemed like a good way... It's much more affordable than renting a car and paying for accommodation, especially when travelling alone. It provides a sense of home when moving all the time; you always have the van that feels like your own place, which is super nice. It was indeed a learning curve, living in the van alone and learning to do everything − fixing the sink, learning to drive a large vehicle − I even got it stuck once! So many crazy things happened; it's rapid personal growth.

Vojo: How do you handle training with all the constraints of living alone in a van?

ZC: There's a lot of prior organisation. If I know it's a big training day, I make sure I've filled the van with water and fuel beforehand and that my bikes are working because I know I'll be super tired when I return. There's also a lot of management, like constantly trying to find a place to park the van, how to repair my bikes, how to buy food, and moving around the city. But it works out once you get into the mindset and accept that you have to spend a bit more time preparing than usual.

Vojo: We often see content about privateer DH or enduro riders, but there are also XC riders who are talked about less. How does it feel to race in the XC World Cup as an independent rider without a team?

ZC: It's true that it's less common in XC. It's challenging because you see teams and all the support they have, even technical support. Whereas for me, most of the time, I have to ask strangers or other people to hand me my bottles during a race. It's a massive contrast, but at the same time, everyone is very welcoming to privateers. It forces you to make friends and meet new people. So many people are ready to help; it's just a bit more effort to get there. And I think privateers are becoming much more recognised. The current World Champion is also a privateer from Oceania (New Zealander Samara Maxwell, who has since joined the RockRider Ford Racing Team).

Vojo: Do you think it would change a lot for you to have a team's support? Or have you found your balance and wouldn't change anything?

ZC: I love travelling in a van, and it's been an incredible experience. But in terms of performance, it's a good way to get to races, but it's probably not optimal. I'll try to find more support for next year. I'd definitely recommend travelling in a van if it's the only option, but I think there's a reason few people do it.

Vojo: It's better to compete in the World Cup in a van than to stay at home, in short.

ZC: Yes, exactly! You have to find a way to be there one way or another.

Vojo: As a privateer, how do you finance the whole season, especially coming from Australia when everything is happening overseas in Europe?

ZC: I have a few partners, but mainly I work. During Covid, we couldn't leave Australia, so I worked as a graphic designer and trail builder. So, when I'm at home, I'm on the trails, and when I can work remotely, I do graphic design. Plus, I created a clothing brand to help fund all of this.

Vojo: I was about to ask. How did you come to launch Rapt Apparel?

ZC: Last year, someone half-jokingly told me I should sell t-shirts. I took it seriously and spent

all of last year planning. I love design, fashion, and creating things, so it seemed a fun challenge. I didn't realise how much work it would be, but again, it's a good learning curve and super cool. At Val di Sole, I saw everyone was in a team, and I wanted one, so we decided to set up our own − Rapt Factory Racing − with a group of friends who also live in their vans for enduro racing. It's pretty funny to say that I sponsor my friends, but yes, it's been fun and a great learning experience.

Vojo: For Europeans who go home between each race, what you're doing is inspiring. Do you keep that in mind?

ZC: Absolutely. I think biking can be somewhat selfish since you know your whole career is that of an athlete, and I think that's something many of my friends who've done it have struggled with finding a way to give back. For me, biking is the way I can give back to the community, and if I can inspire people and show them they can do it, then that's a good thing. Whenever I meet someone who tells me I've helped them or inspired them, it makes my week absolutely great. I would love to be able to give more and try to help more people get into the sport because I think it's super cool.

Check out Zoe's clothing company, Rapt Apparel, at raptapparel.com

Visit our French media friends at vojomag.com

227

E-BIKE WORLD CUP SERIES 2023

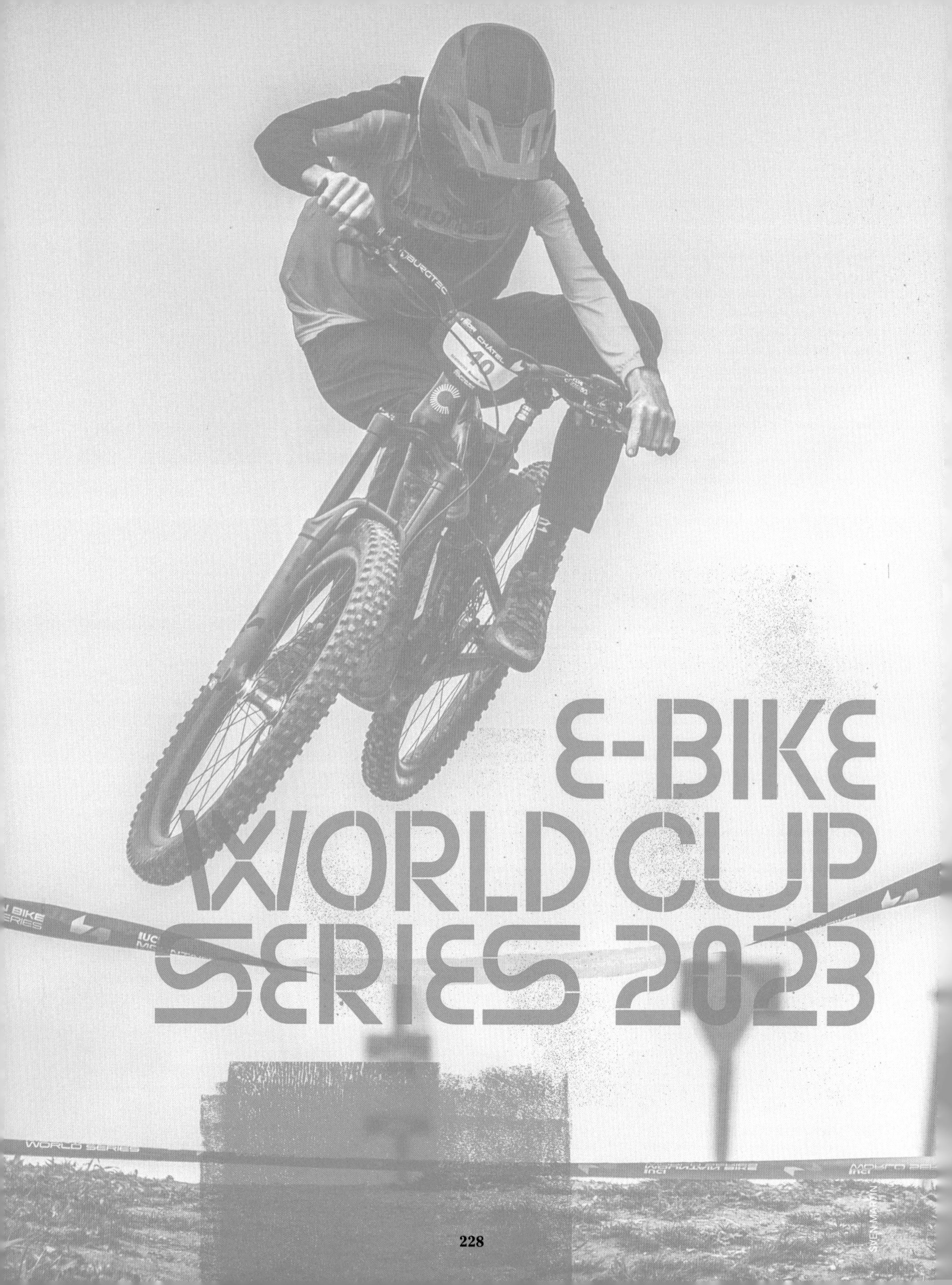

SVEN MARTIN

FULL CHARGE

E-BIKE WORLD CUP SERIES 2023
PIETRA / LEOGANG / VAL DI FASSA /
LOUDENVIELLE / CHÂTEL

In its ten years of competition (2013-2022), the Enduro World Series (EWS) not only created a whole new international race series, but it also helped develop the frames, components and technologies that the majority of mountain bikers now use on every ride. Pre-2013, enduro bikes barely existed; early EWS racers pedalled around with backpacks full of spare parts and multiple helmets (a half-face for climbing, a full-face for descending).

By the end of the series' decade of competition, enduro bikes had become, simply, *mountain bikes*. Enduro had, arguably, been so influential that the bikes people were racing were exactly what everyday riders used and loved – wide range of gears, reliable wheels and tyres (more or less), sturdy frames and plenty of well-damped suspension.

As the EWS became the Enduro World Cup (EDR) in 2023, the renamed events launched with a parallel series of e-bike races, or E-EDRs. The E-EDR series saw five races take place alongside the European rounds of the EDR, and they attracted some big names from other disciplines, as well as a host of fresh talent.

Admittedly, the E-EDR races did sometimes feel a bit like a side-show to the main EDR (entry numbers were in the single digits or tens at every round), but it's impossible to ignore the ever-increasing number of ordinary riders on assisted bikes. With enduro's track record of developing the bikes people ride, and how and where they ride them, it'd be no surprise to see e-bikes morphing into new forms as the E-EDR pushes their limits in future seasons.

The following pages show a selection of highlights from the 2023 E-EDR series.

SEBASTIAN SCHIECK

SEBASTIAN SCHIECK

Below: The contrasting line between the public and private beaches of the beautiful Ligurian coastline, which played host to the opening round of the 2023 E-EDR in Pietra Ligure (part of Finale Outdoor Region). **Opposite:** Ines Thoma made her E-EDR enduro race debut in Pietra and ended the long and hot day in fourth. **Above:** Twenty-one-year-old Antoine Rogge took a break from his downhill World Cup training schedule and finished second.

SVEN MARTIN

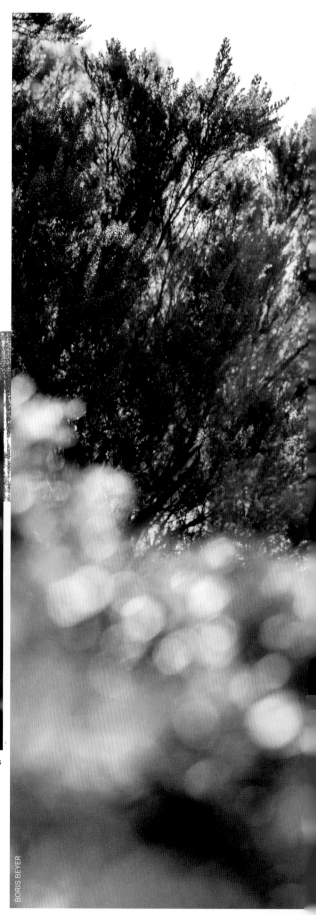

BORIS BEYER

Above: In Pietra Ligure, Fabien Barel became the first men's E-EDR winner – six years after his last world enduro race. **Opposite:** Laura Charles already had a pedigree in world e-bike enduro racing, with four EWS-E wins under her belt. In Pietra she added an E-Enduro World Cup win to her already impressive tally.

BORIS BEYER

SVEN MARTIN

Opposite: Fabien Barel finished Leogang right where he left off in Pietra, taking the win by almost 30 seconds. He looked like the man to beat in 2023. **Top:** SRAM Factory Enduro Racing rider Yannick Pontal couldn't quite find his round one form (where he had finished fourth) and was forced to settle for tenth in Leogang. **Below:** Tracy Moseley took Leogang's opening stage win and then finished second on another six, but this still wasn't enough to best Ines Thoma and secure second place. A mere two seconds separated the two women at the end of the day's proceedings.

Flo Espineira took a big win at round two in Leogang, finishing thirty seconds clear of the rest of the women's field. She secured five stage wins along the way.

SEBASTIAN SCHIECK

SEBASTIAN SCHIECK

SEBASTIAN SCHIECK

Opposite top: Laura Charles took her second E-Enduro World Cup win of 2023 beneath the breathtaking Dolomites. Val di Fassa's jaw-dropping views could not distract her from claiming the race win. **Above:** Despite winning three of the eight stages, Flo Espineira was unable to match Laura Charles for raw speed. The Chilean finished in second place, five seconds back. **Opposite bottom:** Charles' Miranda Factory teammate Tiago Ladeira also had a strong showing, taking an impressive fifth place in Val di Fassa.

"THE 2023 E-EDR WORLD CUP RACED FIVE ROUNDS AT VENUES ACROSS EUROPE"

Opposite: Alex Marin's helmet wasn't the only thing on fire in Val di Fassa. The Spaniard's downhill racing pace and experience lent itself to the long Italian descents and he rode away with second place. **Above:** Hugo Pigeon took some time away from the EDR to race on his e-bike. The swap proved successful as he came third and won two stages. **Below:** Alex Marin.

Fabien Barel had no time to soak in the stunning scenery of his homeland as he only had one thing on his mind: winning. After missing out on the podium at round three, he was hungry for another win in Loudenvielle. Barel won the race by a whopping 38 seconds.

BORIS-BEYER

SEBASTIAN SCHIECK

BORIS BEYER

Above left: Laura Charles found herself on the last step of the podium in Loudenvielle. **Above right:** Mid-run acrobatics. **Opposite top:** (Sik) Mick Hannah added another top-ten finish to what had already been an impressive season for the downhill legend. **Opposite bottom:** A moment of disbelief for Flo Espineira, who claimed her second win of the season. With one round to go, the season overall was within her reach. **Below:** Due to adverse weather conditions, the race organisers were forced to bring the race forward a day. The threat of bad weather didn't stop Mathieu Ruffray from having a good time.

SVEN MARTIN

SVEN MARTIN

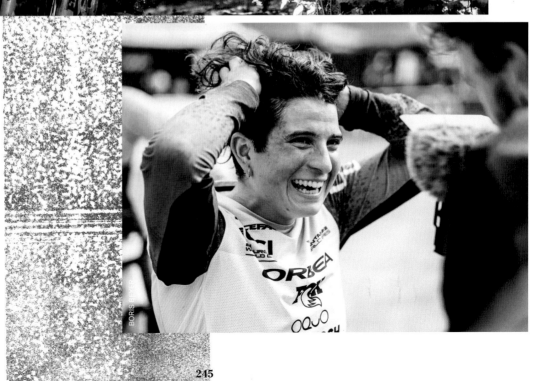

BORIS BEYER

Above: There was no argument, the tracks in Châtel were some of, if not the best the racers had ridden all year. Roost is always the indicator of a good time. **Opposite top:** Just ten points separated Tracy Moseley and Ines Thoma when all was said and done for 2023. Now that is tight racing. **Opposite bottom:** Josh Bryceland brought his combination of style and raw speed to the E-EDR for the final round and finished in an impressive twelfth place.

"AFTER 45 POINTS-WINNING STAGES IN THE SERIES, FABIEN BAREL AND FLO ESPIÑEIRA WON THE E-EDR TITLES"

SEBASTIAN SCHIECK

SVEN MARTIN

SVEN MARTIN

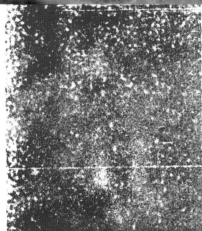

Above: Will Rischbieth powered through Châtel's roots. **Opposite:** A close battle raged between Kevin Marry and Tiago Ladeira all day. However, Marry got ahead in the final stage and claimed the win by a meagre 0.18 seconds. **Below:** Flo Espineira rounded out a consistent year with her third win of the season in Châtel – and took the series title too. Meanwhile, Fabien Barel wrapped up the series title in elite men.

SVEN MARTIN

SERIES STATS:

STAGES	DISTANCE (KM)	DESCENT (M)
45	320.95	18963

TIME CHECK:

OVERALL

Men		Women	
1. Fabien Barel	970	1. Florencia E. Herreros	1254
2. Kevin Marry	929	2. Laura Charles	941
3. Tiago Ladeira	829	3. Ines Thoma	786
4. Alex Marin	673	4. Tracy Moseley	776
5. Michael Hannah	672	5. Sofia Wiedenroth	372

ROUND BY ROUND

ROUND 1
PIETRA LIGURE, ITALY

Men	
1. Fabien Barel	31:51.22
2. Antoine Rogge	+09.40
3. Florian Nicolai	+25.63

Women	
1. Laura Charles	37:02.57
2. F. E. Herreros	+3.82
3. Tracy Moseley	+18.82

ROUND 2
LEOGANG, AUSTRIA

Men	
1. Fabien Barel	36:54.32
2. Michael Hannah	+27.13
3. Tiago Ladeira	+37.24

Women	
1. F. E. Herreros	44:05.33
2. Ines Thoma	+30.81
3. Tracy Moseley	+32.37

ROUND 3
VAL DI FASSA, ITALY

Men	
1. Kevin Marry	40:31.13
2. Alex Marin	+15.31
3. Hugo Pigeon	+22.08

Women	
1. Laura Charles	47:02.74
2. F. E. Herreros	+05.12
3. Ines Thoma	+20.68

ROUND 4
LOUDENVIELLE, FRANCE

Men	
1. Fabien Barel	29:26.50
2. Alex Marin	+38.78
3. Tiago Ladeira	+46.61

Women	
1. F. E. Herreros	35:46.07
2. Tracy Moseley	+16.32
3. Laura Charles	+40.10

ROUND 5
CHÂTEL, FRANCE

Men	
1. Kevin Marry	29:19.88
2. Tiago Ladeira	+00.18
3. Michael Hannah	+06.70

Women	
1. F.E. Herreros	34:46.22
2. Tracy Moseley	+00.04
3. Ines Thoma	+41.17

I Still Have It!

Words: Iago Garay. Images: Sven Martin & Boris Beyer

I've been riding bikes for as long as I can remember. When I first experienced the thrill of riding downhill, it became my favourite part of the ride. After giving racing a go, I fell in love with it and have been racing ever since that moment.

After over ten years of downhill racing and going to the same venues yearly, I was ready for a change. I tried enduro, and it felt refreshing – new venues and trails aplenty each weekend. It reignited my passion for riding. From sharing long climbs with new friends to endless descents and super fun racing, enduro is the complete package. It isn't just about the riding but about the experience.

For the past decade, I've been part of the enduro circuit. However, 2023 was the first time I missed an EWS/Enduro (EDR) World Cup race and had to watch from the sidelines.

It was race day in Pietra Ligure. The third EDR World Cup round was unfolding as expected. Stage one went well. I felt I had a good run and pushed hard. When I finished the stage, I thought, 'That wasn't that hard.' I checked the times, and to my surprise, I didn't go as fast as I thought. It was clear that I needed to step up my speed.

I started the second stage fully committed. Halfway through, something odd happened: I felt pressure in my ears, like when you drive through a tunnel or you're on a plane.' I chuckled and thought, 'I must be going so fast that my ears can't adjust fast enough.' The

pressure kept building until I felt a pop in my ears. I was on a good run, better than the first stage. So, I kept pushing.

A few seconds after the 'pop', I began to develop a throbbing headache, the worst I've ever experienced. I was two-thirds down the stage and desperately wanted to get to the bottom. I suspected a pinched nerve in my neck and devised a plan: reach the finish line, lay on the ground, relax my muscles, and carry on to stage three.

This proved harder than I thought. The pressure in my head was unbearable, and the pain was so intense that I couldn't move it. Nevertheless, I kept going. I was convinced that if I reached the finish line and could lay down, it would all go away, but it didn't. It worsened.

After finishing the stage, I lay on the ground and could barely move. Even the slightest eye movement was excruciatingly painful, so I tried to stay still until the medics arrived. Luckily, the doctor on track quickly identified that I was experiencing an aneurysm.

The following days became a blur. I kept my eyes shut and attempted to sleep as much as possible to cope with the pain. While lying in the hospital bed, waiting for the first surgery, all I could think of was: would I be able to ride my bike again? What if I'm unable to move my limbs? I was utterly terrified. Little did I know that those were the least of my worries. I was fighting for my life.

Two surgeries and a bit of rest mitigated the pain, which enabled me to have a conversation to understand what was happening to me. Ella, my partner, was there throughout, and my parents flew from Spain the day of the incident.

A brain aneurysm can often be fatal, and survivors can frequently grapple with speech and balance issues. Luckily, my quick transfer to the Hospital in Pietra Ligure, which has one of the best neurology teams in Italy, ensured that I received treatment less than two hours after the incident.

I stayed in the hospital for 20 days. Looking back, I have nothing but good memories from my time there. The kindness, love and care of doctors and nurses from the Santa Corona Hospital were crucial in helping me navigate this challenging period. Despite the language barrier, they made every effort to communicate. They would talk to me in broken Spanish, and I would reply in broken Italian. Those short conversations would help me pass the hours until my favourite time of the day, visiting time.

Every day, Ella, my dad and my mom would visit me twice, wearing the brightest smiles to try to hide the pain they were enduring. While my suffering was the worst I've experienced, the uncertainty they were facing was worse.

Barely able to articulate a sentence, all I could do was hold hands, but knowing they were there for me was all I needed. Progressively, I started getting better and could have longer conversations and enjoy their homemade meals.

"The pressure in my head was unbearable, and the pain was so intense that I couldn't move it. Nevertheless, I kept going"

Most of my conversations with Ella revolved around her racing. Instead of chasing the podium, she chose to stay by my side, a decision I will be eternally grateful for. Her strength and love carried me through this ordeal.

The doctors were very pleased with my progress but reminded me to take it easy and give my body time to heal.

After my extended stay in the hospital, my fitness took a dive, and my weight plummeted. The path to recovery would be long. I started with short walks, which progressively became longer. I spent one month walking and visualising myself riding my bike, railing a corner, sending a jump or tackling a rock garden. I remembered the sensations of being on the bike, but at the same time, I feared something had changed and I wouldn't be able to ride the same way again.

In August, after the first check-up with the doctor, I started pedalling on the turbo trainer. The primary concern at that time was exercising in the heat. I wasn't allowed to ride alone in case of any potential problems. So, every morning, I would pedal on the turbo trainer in front of two fans, gradually extending the duration of each session.

Nobody really explained to me how to get back to form after my aneurysm. I think the doctors were cautious in telling me to exercise. Whenever I asked a neurologist for advice, they recommended taking it easy. I took it upon myself and applied the same process and progression

I used to return from an injury: listening to my body, paying attention to my activity recovery and monitoring my heart rate.

It worked, and I made a faster recovery than before. So, Ella and I decided to escape the scorching temperatures in Madrid and go to the Pyrenees. With my favourite training buddy by my side, I resumed my training plan, but this time outdoors. Being able to ride with Ella again was the best motivation I could ask for. Nothing compares to the freedom of being on two wheels.

During our days in the Pyrenees, we drove through the Aran Valley. Outside the biggest town, Vielha, there's a new jump park, and I could see the jumps every time we drove past. One day, I told Ella: 'I think I'm ready to hit some jumps.'

I thought this was the perfect way to get back on a mountain bike – short runs close to the car. With my Jekyll out of the van and my full-face helmet on, I was ready. This was my first time jumping with a heart rate monitor. I had to be careful not to get my heart rate too high. I had to control my excitement and walk slowly up the hill. Once again, I visualised how I wanted to hit the jump and went for it. After over two months without touching a mountain bike, I was back doing what I loved the most, and all my fears disappeared. 'I still have it', I said to myself.

While this was a huge achievement, I still had a long way to return to my previous form.

Luckily, I have the best people by my side, supporting me nonstop, from my sponsors, who understood what I was going through and didn't put me under any pressure, to my family, friends and team.

Ella and Carlos, our mechanic, have been instrumental in helping me regain my skills and speed these past months, from long phone calls and short messages to coming on rides and waiting for me until I got my pace back. Their unwavering support when doubts crept in made the whole process much easier.

After this ordeal, I didn't think my body and my mind would be ready to race at the last two rounds of the EDR World Cup, so I decided to focus on helping the Cannondale Enduro Team perform at their best and have some fun on track while I was at it.

Being back at the races was the last step on this journey. While riding the tracks, I realised again how much I love this sport. The good vibes at the EDR World Cup can't compare to anything else. Seeing everyone again filled my heart with joy; those big hugs we shared will power me for years.

As I write this, I can finally say I'm ready to return to racing at the top level. I have an entire off-season to prepare for it, and I am more excited than ever to put in the hard work. This experience showed me how much I love what I do and my willingness to do anything to stay on the bike surrounded by my friends and family.

Looking back, while I was oblivious to the risk I faced, my body was aware of it. Throughout this ordeal, I wanted to call my friends and tell them how much I loved them. I didn't want to let another day go by without them knowing their importance to me.

I have learnt not to take anything or anyone for granted, as cliché as it may sound. So, make sure you show love to the people you care about. You never know when it will be the last time you see them.

"I realised again how much I love this sport.
The good vibes at the Enduro World Cup can't
compare to anything else"

OVERALL RESULTS

ENDURO WORLD CUP 2023

TOP 20 ELITES

Men	Points
1. Richard Rude	2576
2. Jesse Melamed	2443
3. Alex Rudeau	2395
4. Rhys Verner	2044
5. Charles Murray	1934
6. Youn Deniaud	1850
7. Daniel Booker	1848
8. Slawomir Lukasik	1822
9. Matthew Walker	1647
10. Jack Moir	1526
11. Martin Maes	1364
12. Dimitri Tordo	1352
13. Louis Jeandel	1229
14. José Borges	1228
15. Jack Menzies	1173
16. Zakarias Johansen	1122
17. Brady Stone	1019
18. Elliot Jamieson	989
19. Christian Textor	960
20. Remi Gauvin	940

TOP 20 ELITES

Women	Points
1. Isabeau Courdurier	3183
2. Morgane Charre	3021
3. Harriet Harnden	2333
4. Gloria Scarsi	2061
5. Rebecca Baraona	2012
6. Mélanie Pugin	1787
7. Ella Conolly	1698
8. Rae Morrison	1651
9. Barbora Vojta	1625
10. Noga Korem	1576
11. Raphaela Richter	1409
12. Andreane L. Nadeau	1220
13. Chloe Taylor	1008
14. Julie Duvert	1007
15. Katy Winton	910
16. George Swift	893
17. Polly Henderson	816
18. Nadine Ellecosta	735
19. Amy Morrison	716
20. Helen Weber	610

U21

Men	Points
1. Lisandru Bertini	1120
2. Raphaël Giambi	1003
3. Sascha Kim	995
4. Alexis Icardo	784
5. Johnathan Helly	779

U21

Women	Points
1. Emmy Lan	1224
2. Elly Hoskin	693
3. Lily Planquart	619
4. Erice Van Leuven	462
5. Sophie Riva	448

TEAM STANDINGS

1. Yeti-Fox Factory Race Team	6650
2. Lapierre Zipp Collective	5951
3. Pivot Factory Racing	5294
4. Canyon Cllctv Factory Enduro Team	5023
5. Forbidden Synthesis Team	4682